Digital Dictatorship

How Technology Engineers Obedience Without Force

By

Avery Grant

Vij Books

New Delhi (India)

Published by

Vij Books
(Publishers, Distributors & Importers)
4836/24, 3rd Floor, Ansari Road
Delhi – 110 002
Phone: 91-11-43596460
Mobile: 98110 94883
e-mail: contact@vijpublishing.com
www.vijbooks.in

ISBN: 978-93-90349-89-0 (HB)

ISBN: 978-93-90349-83-8 (PB)

This book was developed using advanced writing tools to support the drafting and ideation process. All content has been thoughtfully curated, refined, and reviewed to ensure quality and relevance.

Contents

Introduction

The New Face of Power

Power has always worn a face. For centuries it bore the features of kings, generals, and presidents, wielding armies, decrees, and punishments. Its presence was unmistakable, felt in the clang of chains, the crack of whips, the spectacle of the guillotine. Authority was legible; resistance, equally so. To be free meant, at least in principle, to escape the visible reach of the sovereign. Today, however, the face of power is harder to discern. It does not reside solely in parliaments, palaces, or corporate boardrooms. Increasingly, it is embedded in the design of systems that we mistake for neutral conveniences—our phones, our online platforms, our payment networks, even the sensors that light our streets or measure our footsteps. Power has become ambient, infrastructural, and quietly persuasive. It no longer shouts commands; it whispers suggestions, organises incentives, and rearranges choices before we even recognise them as such.

This book is about that transformation. It argues that the technologies which once promised emancipation—free speech online, borderless communication, instant access to information—have quietly matured into instruments that can train obedience without overt coercion. The surveillance systems of the past monitored people in order to punish them. The systems of the present monitor us in order to guide us, to "nudge" us, to shape our habits, and ultimately to secure our compliance. The difference is not trivial. Force breeds resistance; invisible design normalises submission. In learning to recognise this new face of power, we are forced to ask uncomfortable questions about what freedom still means in the twenty-first century.

The central claim advanced here is stark but unavoidable: obedience today is engineered not by violence but by architecture. By architecture, I mean not just buildings and roads but the infrastructure of code, data, algorithms, and sensors that surrounds us. The turnstile in a subway station enforces payment more effectively than a guard with a baton. A digital reputation score disciplines behaviour more efficiently than a court trial. An algorithm that determines which posts we see online shapes our worldview more decisively than any censor's pen. Power has shifted from visible acts of domination to invisible systems of design. It has become embedded in the choices we believe we make freely.

This shift matters not only for those who live under authoritarian regimes but also for those who believe they live within robust democracies. It is tempting to imagine that the techniques of digital control belong exclusively to Beijing or Moscow, to authoritarianism's heavy hand. But to do so is to miss the deeper convergence taking place. The same principles that underpin China's Social Credit System—rewarding "good" citizens and penalising "bad"—can be found, albeit in subtler forms, in the Uber driver's star rating, the FICO score that determines access to loans, or the algorithm that decides which job applications make it past an employer's digital gatekeeping system. Democracies may not deploy the same rhetoric, but they increasingly adopt the same logics. The consequence is a new global order of obedience by design, in which cultural and ideological differences mask a shared reliance on digital architectures of control.

The urgency of the problem becomes clear when we acknowledge the speed at which these systems spread. Once developed, technologies of surveillance and behavioural steering travel easily across borders, industries, and political systems. American firms pioneer targeted advertising; Chinese firms refine mass social scoring; European governments experiment with digital IDs and biometric databases. Each borrows from the other. Police departments in the United States purchase predictive policing software whose logic resembles the "Minority Report" fictions of popular culture. Corporations in the West eagerly export surveillance tools to regimes abroad. And as the COVID-19 pandemic demonstrated, entire populations can be trained within months to accept health monitoring, location tracing, and digital checkpoints—all under the language of protection and responsibility. The lesson is clear: the line between democracy and dictatorship, when it comes to digital control, is far thinner than we imagine.

Why is this shift so powerful? Because it makes obedience feel voluntary. When people obey laws out of fear of punishment, they remain aware of their submission. When they follow a rule because their app rewarded them with points, or because default settings guided them toward a particular option, they believe they are exercising free will. This is the genius of modern systems of control: they manufacture compliance by aligning incentives, shaping habits, and presenting carefully engineered choices. To the individual, the decision appears natural; to the system, the behaviour is predictable. The citizen, consumer, or worker rarely feels coerced. They feel empowered, connected, even gratified—precisely because the mechanisms of control are disguised as conveniences.

Consider how daily life has already been transformed by this quiet architecture. A gig economy worker maintains their star rating with a vigilance once reserved for religious observance, aware that a dip below five stars may cost them their livelihood. A student completes coursework on a platform that logs every keystroke, conditioning diligence not through punishment but through constant visibility. A parent installs monitoring apps on their child's phone, teaching the next generation that surveillance is normal, even protective. Meanwhile, households fill with devices—thermostats, cameras, speakers—that listen, record, and subtly shape routines. None of these examples requires the violence of the state. Yet all discipline behaviour with remarkable effectiveness.

The challenge is that these systems work too well. Human beings are creatures of habit and reward; we respond to incentives faster than to ideology. Bread and circuses pacified populations in ancient Rome; Amazon Prime and personalised feeds pacify them today. The technologies of convenience seduce us into trading autonomy for ease, rarely pausing to calculate the cost. We tell ourselves that we are free because we can click, swipe, or speak a command. Yet those choices are already framed, narrowed, and preconditioned by architectures invisible to us. The question is no longer whether we are free in the abstract, but whether our freedom has been quietly redefined to mean nothing more than efficient conformity within the system.

This book is not the first to examine surveillance, but it seeks to approach the problem differently. Much of the literature remains trapped in binaries: authoritarian versus democratic, East versus West, liberty versus repression. These frames miss the deeper continuity. What unites the credit rating in the United States with the social credit experiment in China, or the biometric checkpoints of India with the predictive policing of Britain, is not shared ideology but shared logic. Both democracies and dictatorships increasingly rely on data-driven systems that pre-empt behaviour, enforce conformity, and render deviation costly. This convergence demands a new lens: one that does not excuse the excesses of authoritarian regimes, but also does not allow liberal democracies to imagine themselves immune.

The question is not simply who controls the technology, but how the technology itself restructures the possibilities of control.

The analysis that follows will trace this transformation across multiple dimensions. It will show how the tools of power have shifted from punishment to incentives, from visible repression to hidden design. It will explore how choice itself is engineered, how predictive systems discipline unpredictability, and how gamified platforms train obedience under the guise of play. It will examine how cultural narratives—safety, efficiency, progress—mask deeper structures of surveillance, and how economics binds states and corporations together in the pursuit of data. It will assess why resistance often fails, why outrage dissipates, and why even the most heroic disclosures rarely disrupt the system's expansion. And it will situate these developments historically, showing both the continuities with past forms of domination and the radical novelties of our digital moment.

The reader is invited to approach this book not simply as a catalogue of abuses but as a framework for rethinking freedom itself. Freedom, in this age, cannot mean the absence of oversight; nor can it mean the naïve embrace of every technological advance. Instead, it must mean the capacity to navigate systems consciously, to preserve unpredictability, and to cultivate spaces where conformity is not the default condition. The task is not merely to denounce technology but to understand its logics, to recognise where obedience is being engineered, and to imagine alternatives that preserve human agency. If freedom is to survive, it must be redefined for a world where control has ceased to be spectacular and has become banal, where power is not a face we can confront but an architecture we inhabit.

The stakes are high. The societies that master obedience without force will appear stable, prosperous, and efficient. Their citizens will mistake compliance for contentment. Yet beneath that surface lies the risk of a humanity too predictable, too docile, too engineered to resist. What makes us human—our creativity, our unpredictability, our refusal to be wholly legible—may be the last frontier worth defending. This book offers no simple answers. But it does offer a lens through which to see the new face of power, and a call to recognise that our freedom, if it is to mean anything, must resist being reduced to an algorithmic calculation.

We stand, then, at a crossroads. Not one marked by revolution or coup, but by the quiet consolidation of systems that reshape our choices before we know we are making them. The challenge is to see these systems for what they are, to resist the seductions of convenience, and to ask anew what it means to live freely in a world where control requires no chains. This is the story of our digital age—not one of overt tyranny, but of a dictatorship that governs through design, not decree. To understand it is the first step toward resisting it.

Chapter 1

The End of Visible Chains

For much of human history, power announced itself with unmistakable clarity. To disobey the sovereign was to risk the sword, the noose, the cell, or the scaffold. Streets and squares bore witness to the rituals of punishment designed not only to discipline the offender but to terrify the onlooker. The guillotine's blade, the gulag's labour, the prison's bars—these were symbols of authority that brooked no ambiguity. Rule was upheld by force, and freedom was defined by the ability to slip its grip. Yet the modern citizen walks through cities without seeing public executions, forced labour camps, or even a heavy police presence. Instead, the discipline that once required steel and blood now seems to operate without spectacle, without visible threat. This chapter begins with a paradox: control has not disappeared, it has been re-engineered. Where rulers once coerced, systems now incentivise. Where chains once clanked, data now flows. Where punishment once loomed, algorithms now nudge.

The transition from violence to incentives is not merely a technical upgrade in governance; it is a fundamental reorganisation of how power operates on human beings. Consider the difference between the guillotine and the credit score. The guillotine compels obedience through fear of annihilation. The credit score achieves compliance through the promise of access—better loans, cheaper mortgages, smoother participation in economic life. Both ensure order, but one through terror, the other through reward. The gulag breaks the body to enforce submission; the user rating conditions behaviour by subtly disciplining service providers into cheerful conformity. If the guillotine represents the sovereign's power to decide who may live and who must die, the credit score represents the system's power to decide who may participate and who must be excluded. In both cases, the stakes are existential, but the mechanisms could not be more different. Fear paralyses; incentives mobilise. And for modern governance, mobilisation proves far more effective than mere deterrence.

What makes this shift so potent is that rewards, unlike punishments, often appear voluntary. A driver working for a ride-hailing platform carefully tends to their star rating, not because the state commands it, but because customers, through the silent medium of digital feedback, determine their livelihood. A citizen pays taxes not only to avoid prosecution but also to access benefits, services, and credits that make life smoother. A consumer agrees to terms and conditions not under duress but for the promise of free shipping, exclusive access, or points that accumulate invisibly into privileges. The guillotine produces resistance, rebellion, and martyrdom; the credit score produces self-discipline, self-censorship, and self-monitoring. In one case, disobedience is crushed from without; in the other, obedience grows from within.

The architecture of this new obedience is rarely acknowledged because it is rarely visible. Apps, platforms, and surveillance cameras form the skeleton of a society in which behaviour is shaped before the law ever intervenes. The door lock that requires a digital key, the subscription service that auto-renews, the recommendation feed that personalises content—all structure choices in ways that govern behaviour invisibly. Michel Foucault, writing about prisons, coined the term "disciplinary architecture" to describe how physical spaces could enforce compliance more effectively than guards. Today's disciplinary architecture is less about stone and steel and more about code and design. A simple example illustrates this: jaywalking in a major city may technically be a minor offence punishable by fine. Yet if the pedestrian crossing is designed with barriers, signals, and surveillance cameras linked to facial recognition, the opportunity for disobedience disappears. The system conditions obedience not through punishment after the fact but through the impossibility of deviation in the first place. This is governance not through decree but through design.

The Chinese Social Credit System is perhaps the most vivid illustration of this principle. Popularly caricatured as a dystopian score that dictates whether citizens may travel, borrow, or participate in society, its reality is more fragmented but equally instructive. Pilot projects link financial reliability, legal compliance, and even social behaviour to a composite assessment of trustworthiness. Citizens who pay debts on time, support family members, and behave courteously may enjoy easier access to loans, priority in school admissions, or cheaper transport fares. Those who default on obligations, violate regulations, or spread misinformation may find themselves restricted from booking high-speed trains or flights, their names published on lists of dishonour, or their children denied prestigious school placements. The genius—and danger—of such a system lies in its subtlety. Unlike the gulag, it does not need to break bodies. Unlike the guillotine, it does not need to end lives. Instead, it creates a regime where deviation from prescribed norms results not in death but in exclusion, inconvenience, and social stigma. Citizens internalise the rules, adjusting their behaviour proactively to avoid falling behind. And while Western audiences may recoil, the echoes are uncomfortably familiar: the Uber driver striving for five stars, the employee optimising their LinkedIn profile for algorithmic visibility, the consumer maintaining a FICO score to secure basic financial participation. The mechanism differs in scope, but the logic is shared.

What unites these examples is the core idea of obedience without violence. The most effective systems of control today do not parade their authority; they embed it in routines. They do not rely on spectacle; they rely on subtle reinforcement. To disobey is no longer to risk the axe but to risk invisibility, exclusion, or diminished opportunity. And herein lies the difficulty: resistance is harder to mobilise when repression is not visible. Protest against executions or mass imprisonment finds ready audiences because the violence is undeniable. Protest against algorithmic opacity or credit scoring attracts far less solidarity, even though the long-term effects may be just as corrosive to freedom. Citizens rarely march in the streets over the architecture of an app or the logic of a database, yet those are the very infrastructures through which behaviour is being reshaped. The guillotine created martyrs; the credit score creates compliant consumers.

This chapter invites the reader to think critically about this shift in the mechanics of power. It will trace how societies moved from visible chains—punishments, prisons, executions—to invisible architectures of incentives, ratings, and predictive systems. It will explore the infrastructures that condition behaviour before law or force are even applied, demonstrating how design has become the true mechanism of governance. It will examine the Chinese Social Credit System as both a futuristic experiment and a mirror reflecting the trajectories of Western societies. And it will advance the central argument of this book: that the most formidable systems of control now operate without overt violence, making resistance not impossible but profoundly more complex. Obedience is no longer demanded; it is cultivated. And if we are to understand what freedom might mean today, we must first learn to recognise the invisible chains that bind us as effectively as any prison once did.

From Violence to Incentives

The story of power has always been, at its core, a story of obedience. For centuries, rulers secured compliance by making disobedience synonymous with pain, exile, or death. The guillotine did not simply punish a criminal; it dramatised the cost of defiance for all who watched. The gulag did not merely incapacitate political opponents; it reminded millions that to step out of line was to be erased into silence and cold. These instruments of coercion were explicit, theatrical, and visible. They created a world in which fear was both the glue of social order and the measure of political control. Yet as societies have evolved, the spectacle of violence has given way to subtler, more insidious mechanisms. Today, the citizen does not need to be flogged into obedience; they are conditioned through systems of reward, credit, and access. The guillotine has been replaced by the credit score, the gulag by the algorithmic rating. Power still ensures conformity, but it now does so through invisible incentives rather than visible chains.

The reason for this transformation is not moral enlightenment but practical efficiency. Violence is a blunt instrument. It shocks populations into compliance, but it also breeds resentment, resistance, and, eventually, revolt. History is littered with empires undone by their own brutality: Rome's spectacles of blood that bred disdain among its subjects, or the Soviet Union's gulags that generated an underground culture of dissent despite the omnipresence of fear. Coercion is high-maintenance; it demands constant surveillance, a large apparatus of enforcers, and endless resources to sustain punishment. Incentives, by contrast, achieve the same result at a fraction of the cost. A citizen who polices themselves to maintain a positive financial rating or a flawless professional reputation is infinitely easier to govern than one who must be threatened into compliance. A consumer who willingly trades personal data for loyalty points or discounts is far more manageable than one forced to surrender information at gunpoint. *Incentives economise power by internalising it.*

This shift also reflects the changing nature of what societies value. In the eighteenth and nineteenth centuries, power was demonstrated by the sovereign's ability to decide over life and death. Public executions and mass imprisonment reaffirmed the state's supremacy. Today, the stakes of inclusion and exclusion are tied less to survival and more to participation in systems of consumption and mobility. To be denied access to credit, to lose a platform rating, to fall into algorithmic invisibility—these are the modern equivalents of exile. They do not extinguish life, but they render life progressively unliveable in societies where access is mediated by digital infrastructures. A low credit score can mean no home, no loan, no future. A poor rating can mean no work, no visibility, no income. *Obedience is thus secured not through terror of dying but through fear of being excluded from the privileges that make life viable.*

The rise of platforms has normalised this logic in ways most people rarely reflect upon. A restaurant that slips below four stars on a review site struggles to attract customers, even if its food and service remain unchanged. A driver with less than five stars may be sidelined by algorithms that favour higher-rated competitors, effectively locking them out of income opportunities. A user whose profile appears unreliable to a dating app's matching system finds themselves deprived of visibility and choice, regardless of their real character or intentions. None of these consequences involves violence, yet they are profoundly coercive. They channel behaviour towards conformity: smile more at passengers, offer free mints, suppress honest criticism in reviews, and self-curate relentlessly online. The theatre of punishment has been replaced by the quiet tyranny of feedback loops.

What distinguishes this modern architecture of control is that it rarely feels imposed. Citizens submit to credit checks, users crave high ratings, consumers chase reward points—not because they are visibly coerced, but because the systems promise benefits. Here lies the genius of incentives: they disguise obedience as aspiration. Where violence instils fear, incentives inspire hope. Yet both are equally binding. In fact, incentives are often more powerful precisely because they are less recognisable as tools of domination. A political prisoner in Stalin's Russia knew they were being punished by the state. A citizen in a modern democracy, denied a loan due to opaque scoring systems, may never recognise the political nature of their exclusion. The chains have been internalised, hidden within the structures of normal economic and social life.

One may be tempted to celebrate this as progress: fewer executions, fewer prisons, less overt brutality. And indeed, on a surface level, the decline of violence in governance is a triumph of human civilisation. Yet it would be naïve to confuse the disappearance of visible coercion with the disappearance of control. The very fact that incentives produce less resistance makes them more formidable. It is easy to rally public outrage against mass killings or forced labour camps. It is far harder to galvanise protest against a points-based consumer loyalty programme or a digital feedback system, even when these operate as mechanisms of control just as surely as the lash once did. *The absence of blood does not mean the absence of domination; it means domination has become less visible, more intimate, and more difficult to resist.*

Historically, the transition from punishment to incentive can be traced alongside the evolution of capitalism itself. Industrial-era societies required disciplined workers, reliable borrowers, and obedient citizens. The state and the market discovered that compliance could be secured not only through prisons and executions but through wages, access to credit, and reputational systems. Max Weber described the "iron cage" of rational bureaucracy, where rules and procedures disciplined individuals as effectively as physical chains. Today, that cage has been digitised. The rules are no longer written in dusty ledgers but in lines of code. The bureaucrat's stamp has been replaced by the algorithm's calculation. And yet the function remains the same: to regulate behaviour in ways that ensure predictability, reliability, and control.

The tension at the heart of this system is that incentives often feel indistinguishable from freedom. To choose to obey for the sake of a reward appears voluntary, even empowering. The gig worker who adjusts their behaviour to preserve a five-star rating believes they are exercising entrepreneurial agency. The student who strives for perfect attendance to maintain eligibility for scholarships views their compliance as self-discipline. Yet the boundaries of their choices have been carefully engineered. Rewards are structured to guide behaviour in predetermined directions. What masquerades as freedom is often nothing more than a carefully curated menu of options designed to elicit conformity. As behavioural economists have demonstrated, the framing of choices profoundly affects decisions; the "default setting" is often the most powerful form of governance. When obedience is engineered through incentives, citizens feel free even as they are being managed.

The philosophical stakes of this transformation are profound. Violence, for all its brutality, at least made the structure of power visible. It forced societies to confront the question of legitimacy: who has the right to punish, and on what grounds? Incentives obscure these questions by making compliance feel consensual. Who, after all, would protest against a system that rewards "good" behaviour? Yet this obscurity is precisely what makes the new logic of power so dangerous. When the architecture of control is embedded in apps, ratings, and scores, the political character of these mechanisms is disguised as neutral, technical, or inevitable. Resistance becomes harder not only because the penalties are less dramatic, but because the very need to resist is less recognisable.

The journey from the guillotine to the credit score is therefore not simply a shift in methods but a redefinition of what it means to govern. Violence disciplined bodies; incentives discipline behaviour at the level of desire, aspiration, and choice. One worked through fear of death; the other works through fear of exclusion. Both ensure obedience, but incentives achieve it with greater efficiency, broader reach, and deeper penetration into the fabric of daily life. The citizen of the past looked over their shoulder for the guard. The citizen of today looks down at their rating, their score, their digital reputation—and adjusts their behaviour accordingly. The chain no longer rattles, but it holds firm.

The Hidden Architecture of Control

The most powerful forms of control rarely announce themselves. They are built into the background, woven into routines so familiar that they are mistaken for neutral conveniences rather than instruments of governance. Laws can be challenged, police officers can be confronted, but the design of infrastructure works at a deeper level. It shapes behaviour before the law is invoked, before force is required, and often before individuals even recognise they are being directed. The traffic light does not punish jaywalking; it structures movement. The turnstile does not criminalise non-payment; it makes passage impossible without compliance. In the digital age, these mechanisms have multiplied and migrated into platforms, apps, and networks that condition our choices, subtly but systematically. This is the hidden architecture of control: a governance not of edicts but of design.

The distinction matters because visible repression invites resistance. Citizens confronted with overt censorship, curfews, or patrols are acutely aware of their constraints. Yet when restrictions are embedded in the logic of a platform or the default setting of a device, resistance is harder to articulate. Consider how apps determine the rhythms of daily life. A ride-hailing driver does not need a supervisor hovering nearby; their performance is monitored, scored, and ranked by software that dictates how often they are assigned trips and what earnings they can expect. The architecture of the app enforces standards more effectively than a human manager ever could. Similarly, the user of a social media platform experiences a feed curated by algorithms designed to maximise engagement. The choice of what to view is framed as individual autonomy, yet the menu has already been filtered, ranked, and prioritised. This is governance by infrastructure: a regime of behavioural nudging so embedded that it masquerades as freedom.

Surveillance cameras provide another illustration of how design reshapes conduct. When the panopticon was first theorised by Jeremy Bentham, its power lay in making individuals believe they were always being observed. Modern cameras take this further, not only recording but increasingly recognising, analysing, and predicting. The installation of closed-circuit television across London, for example, has not simply created a network of watchers but has normalised constant visibility. Citizens adapt their behaviour in anticipation of being monitored. The cameras rarely intervene directly; their mere presence conditions compliance. This is the essence of infrastructural control: *it reduces the need for explicit enforcement by making disobedience unthinkable or impractical in the first place.*

The language of design obscures the political nature of these systems. User-friendly interfaces, personalised experiences, and seamless transactions are presented as value-neutral improvements. Yet beneath the surface lies a logic of governance. The auto-renewal setting on a subscription service is framed as convenience but functions as a mechanism of capture, ensuring ongoing payment unless the user actively resists. The navigation app that reroutes traffic away from certain neighbourhoods is described as efficient but subtly redistributes flows of people and capital, shaping urban life in ways few notice. Even mundane features such as the placement of buttons, the structure of menus, and the ranking of search results embody decisions about what behaviours to encourage and which to discourage. Infrastructure is never neutral; it encodes priorities and enforces norms. The politics of design are no less consequential than the politics of law.

China's Social Credit System demonstrates how these mechanisms can be scaled into explicit governance frameworks. Although often misunderstood in the West as a single, unified score, the reality is a patchwork of local experiments and sectoral programmes. What unites them is the principle of embedding behavioural incentives into infrastructure. A citizen who repays loans promptly may receive privileges such as expedited travel, while one who defaults may find themselves unable to book flights or access certain services. No policeman drags them away, no court convicts them of treason. The system works by embedding rewards and penalties directly into the platforms that mediate daily life. Western observers may recoil, yet echoes are already present in rating systems that shape everything from creditworthiness to employability. The logic is the same: infrastructure as discipline, design as governance.

What makes invisible design so effective is that it does not feel imposed. Individuals believe they are making choices, unaware that those choices have been framed in advance. Behavioural economics has demonstrated the power of "choice architecture"—the way in which the structuring of options profoundly influences decisions. A pension scheme with an automatic enrolment default achieves far higher participation rates than one requiring active sign-up. The difference is not in law or force but in design. Applied across digital infrastructures, such logic governs millions of micro-decisions daily, nudging populations toward compliance without the friction of overt coercion. *The brilliance of invisible design is that it turns governance into habit.*

Yet to describe this architecture as hidden does not mean it is secret. On the contrary, it is visible in every interface, every camera, every rating system. What makes it hidden is our tendency to naturalise it, to mistake it for the background conditions of modern life. We notice censorship when a book is banned, but not when a search engine quietly deprioritises dissenting content. We notice policing when officers patrol the streets, but not when predictive algorithms redirect resources to certain neighbourhoods, shaping perceptions of criminality before any law is applied. The invisibility lies in normalisation. To live surrounded by infrastructure is to stop noticing its presence, even as it governs us more intimately than decrees ever could.

There are those who argue that this is simply the benign logic of efficiency: systems designed to reduce friction, to streamline decisions, to make life easier. But efficiency is never neutral. The drive to optimise is always aligned with particular interests—corporate profitability, state security, social conformity. The convenience of one-click purchasing benefits consumers but also entrenches monopolies and encourages compulsive consumption. The ease of biometric access speeds travel but also builds databases of unprecedented scope. The rhetoric of seamlessness masks the reality of control. When infrastructure becomes the medium of governance, the boundaries of freedom are redrawn not by laws debated in parliaments but by design choices made in boardrooms and coding sprints.

The philosophical challenge posed by this architecture is that it shifts the locus of power. Sovereignty once resided visibly in rulers and institutions; today, it resides in systems whose operation is often opaque. A citizen can vote out a government but cannot easily challenge the algorithm that curates their news feed. They can protest against police brutality but find it harder to protest against predictive policing software that assigns risk scores to neighbourhoods. The law can be contested in court, but the design of platforms is shielded as proprietary. The centre of gravity has moved from decree to design, from visible authority to invisible architecture. To speak of governance now requires us to pay as much attention to the structures of code and infrastructure as to the texts of constitutions or the speeches of leaders.

Recognising the hidden architecture of control requires a shift in perception. It demands that we see design not merely as technical or aesthetic, but as political. It calls for an awareness that the background systems of life—apps, platforms, cameras, defaults—are not passive but active forces shaping conduct. And it forces us to confront the unsettling truth that in many cases, the most decisive governance does not take the form of a law we can debate or a punishment we can protest, but of an interface we accept without question. The hidden architecture of control is not the absence of politics; it is politics by other means, embedded in the very infrastructures that make modern life possible.

Case Study: The Social Credit System

Few policy experiments in recent history have generated as much fascination, alarm, and misunderstanding as China's Social Credit System. Launched in embryonic form in the early 2010s and gradually rolled out through pilots across cities and provinces, it was often described by foreign media as a dystopian score that reduced the complexity of citizenship to a single number. The reality is less monolithic, yet no less significant. Rather than one unified programme, the Social Credit System is a constellation of initiatives—some run by local governments, others by private firms—that share a common aim: to use digital records of behaviour to reward compliance and punish deviation. What distinguishes it from older systems of policing or credit assessment is the ambition to fold every domain of life—financial, legal, social, even moral—into a single framework of evaluation. The vision is not simply to monitor, but to engineer trustworthiness in a society that the state often frames as suffering from a deficit of honesty and reliability.

To understand the significance of this system, one must recognise its dual nature. On the one hand, it is an attempt to modernise governance in a rapidly digitising society. China's leaders have long worried about fraud, corruption, and weak enforcement of contracts. Courts struggle with the sheer volume of disputes, local officials often act inconsistently, and many citizens distrust commercial and institutional actors alike. By centralising information about debts, contracts, fines, and legal obligations, the Social Credit System promises to fill these gaps. On the other hand, the system extends far beyond the technical task of improving creditworthiness.

It links legal compliance with social reputation, turning trust into a comprehensive currency. A company that fails to pay workers on time may be blacklisted, while an individual who violates court orders may be restricted from purchasing flights or high-speed train tickets. To be trustworthy is not merely to be financially reliable; it is to embody a wide spectrum of behaviours deemed desirable by the state.

What makes the system so striking is its use of incentives rather than overt punishments. Citizens who demonstrate positive behaviour—such as timely repayment of debts, community service, or even volunteering in public campaigns—can receive perks ranging from faster processing of permits to preferential access to schools or healthcare. Conversely, those who fail to comply with legal or contractual obligations may find themselves on public lists of "dishonest persons," facing not prison but restrictions that complicate daily life. The penalties are designed to sting without being brutal: denial of luxury consumption, slowed bureaucratic processes, or reputational shaming through publication of names online. In this way, the Social Credit System functions less like a policeman's baton and more like an algorithmic filter, gradually excluding the "untrustworthy" from the conveniences of modern society. *The true power lies not in punishing infractions, but in incentivising conformity across a wide behavioural spectrum.*

International critics often cast this as a uniquely authoritarian project, and in some respects it is. The system is aligned with the Chinese Communist Party's longstanding priority of social harmony, reinforcing collective norms over individual autonomy. It also reflects a governance style that privileges surveillance and pre-emptive control over negotiation and dissent. Yet to dismiss it as alien obscures its unsettling familiarity. The Uber driver who fears that one low rating may jeopardise their livelihood, or the American borrower whose credit score determines access to housing, employment, and mobility, is living under a parallel logic. Both are systems in which reputation becomes a form of currency, and in which digital infrastructure distributes rewards and penalties without direct human oversight. The Social Credit System may be more ambitious in scope, but its core mechanism—the algorithmic governance of trust—is already embedded in Western societies under different names.

The infrastructure enabling such governance deserves close attention. Local pilots in China have used data drawn from courts, tax offices, financial institutions, and sometimes social media platforms to build individual and corporate profiles. Citizens are not only scored on economic behaviour but also on whether they pay fines promptly, honour contracts, or comply with judicial decisions. Businesses face assessments of tax compliance, environmental responsibility, and even product quality. Those deemed reliable gain green channels through bureaucracy; those deemed unreliable encounter obstacles that slow them down. The system thus moves away from reactive enforcement—punishing after the fact—and towards anticipatory conditioning, where the very design of participation makes compliance the path of least resistance. This is the essence of invisible governance: rather than threatening to punish disobedience, it rewards behaviours that minimise friction within the system.

The appeal for policymakers is evident. Traditional enforcement is costly, requiring armies of bureaucrats and police officers. Incentive-based governance, by contrast, scales through data infrastructure. An algorithm can blacklist thousands of defaulters in seconds, restrict their access to travel, and broadcast their names across multiple platforms. No trials or cells are necessary. The shame of being labelled "dishonest" by the system, combined with the inconveniences imposed, pushes many to comply voluntarily. Herein lies the efficiency: individuals discipline themselves in anticipation of penalties or in pursuit of rewards. Compliance is cultivated internally, reducing the need for external coercion. *The architecture of governance is embedded in the everyday, not enforced at the margins by force.*

Of course, the Social Credit System is not without resistance or critique inside China. Some citizens question its fairness, noting that errors in data can have disproportionate consequences. Others worry that the system privileges loyalty to official narratives over genuine trustworthiness. Scholars point out that transparency and accountability remain weak, making it difficult for individuals to challenge or correct their status. Yet these criticisms have not prevented the steady expansion of pilots and the consolidation of the system's principles into national planning documents. For many ordinary citizens, the benefits—greater predictability in commerce, reduced fraud, streamlined bureaucratic processes—outweigh the abstract risks. In a society accustomed to rapid modernisation and prone to distrust in both markets and institutions, the promise of a more reliable social order carries real appeal.

Contrasting perspectives illuminate why the Social Credit System remains a lightning rod of global debate. For its defenders, it is a rational extension of digital governance, addressing problems of dishonesty and weak enforcement that plague developing economies. For its detractors, it is a chilling prototype of totalitarianism, embedding political loyalty into the metrics of daily life. Both perspectives are correct to some extent, but both risk missing the larger picture. What makes the system significant is not only its local particularities but its embodiment of a broader shift: the migration of governance from visible law and punishment into invisible design and infrastructure. The lesson is not that China is uniquely repressive, but that the tools of algorithmic compliance are converging globally, whether in the name of efficiency, trust, or convenience.

For Western readers, the most unsettling recognition may be that the distance between Beijing's social credit pilots and their own digital environments is smaller than it seems. Every time a platform ranks a user, every time a credit score determines access, every time a loyalty programme rewards predictable behaviour, the logic of digital governance deepens. China's Social Credit System makes explicit what in other societies remains fragmented and disguised: that digital architectures are no longer neutral utilities but active instruments of behavioural conditioning. The question is not whether such systems will shape the future, but how consciously societies will choose to engage with them. The Social Credit System is less a foreign curiosity than a mirror, reflecting the trajectory of governance in a digital world where obedience is engineered not through violence, but through the quiet logic of incentives, ratings, and reputation.

The Core Idea of Obedience Without Violence

History is littered with images of authority exerted through brutality—soldiers lining the streets, gallows erected in town squares, prisons swelling with dissenters. For centuries, power legitimised itself through spectacle, demonstrating its capacity to wound, confine, or destroy those who resisted it. Yet the great paradox of our present moment is that obedience has never been so thorough, so deeply internalised, and yet so rarely accompanied by violence. Control has not vanished; it has dissolved into infrastructures, incentives, and interfaces that render compliance the most natural course of action. What makes this transformation striking is not only its subtlety but its effectiveness: people do not feel coerced, yet they behave as though they were. *The most powerful systems of domination are those that no longer need to raise their voice.*

The shift from repression to conditioning can be seen most clearly in the design of everyday life. The citizen is no longer confronted by the policeman's baton, but by the login requirement that bars access until conditions are met. The consumer is not dragged to court for failure to pay, but automatically excluded from credit-based services if their financial profile falls short. The worker is not berated by a manager for lack of productivity; instead, their dashboard quietly ranks them against colleagues, nudging them into greater effort out of fear of falling behind. In each case, behaviour is shaped, not through visible punishment, but through systems that make certain choices easy, others difficult, and still others impossible. Force becomes unnecessary because the infrastructure itself dictates compliance.

The genius of this model lies in its invisibility. When people are compelled by violence, they know they are being dominated. A society that sees tanks in the streets cannot mistake its condition. But when compliance is engineered through invisible design, the lines between autonomy and coercion blur. A social media user who self-censors for fear of losing followers experiences their behaviour as a personal choice, even though it is shaped by platform incentives. A student who attends every class to maintain a digital attendance record believes they are disciplined by their own will, while in fact they are responding to a system that links their participation to eligibility for exams or scholarships. Invisibility makes resistance harder because the very need to resist appears absent.

Real-world systems demonstrate this logic with unsettling clarity. Consider predictive policing software in the United States. By funnelling officers into certain neighbourhoods based on algorithmic predictions of crime, the system effectively creates self-fulfilling cycles: more patrols generate more arrests, reinforcing the prediction. Citizens in these areas live under a heavier shadow of surveillance, not because of explicit political decree, but because invisible systems allocate resources in ways that entrench disadvantage. The repression is real, yet the mechanism is hidden in data and code rather than soldiers and shackles. Similarly, in the workplace, monitoring software records keystrokes, webcam activity, and output rates, conditioning employees to optimise their productivity. Few protests emerge, not because the monitoring is benign, but because it is framed as efficiency rather than coercion. *Where power is invisible, it is also insulated from contestation.*

It is tempting to assume that societies without overt repression are freer, but the reality is more complicated. Freedom is not simply the absence of visible chains; it is the capacity to act unpredictably, to deviate without disproportionate consequence. Systems of invisible control narrow that capacity by making deviation costly, inefficient, or impossible. Citizens do not feel the lash, but they feel the silent penalties of exclusion—denial of access, diminished opportunities, reputational harm. In China's social credit experiments, "untrustworthy" citizens are not jailed but barred from booking train tickets, their names circulated publicly, their children denied certain schools. In Western contexts, the logic is subtler but familiar: a low credit score restricts financial opportunities; a poor rating on a platform undermines one's livelihood; an opaque algorithm quietly downgrades one's visibility in professional networks. These systems operate without violence, but their grip is no less constraining.

The psychological dimension of obedience without violence is crucial. When individuals perceive their compliance as self-chosen, they are less likely to rebel. A prisoner resists their jailer because they know they are being constrained; a consumer embraces a loyalty scheme because they feel rewarded, even as it locks them into predictable patterns. By aligning control with aspiration, invisible systems eliminate the sense of coercion. People discipline themselves, often more rigorously than they would under threat. This is why incentives, ratings, and gamification prove so effective: they transform control into desire, obedience into habit. *The most profound domination occurs not when people are forced to obey, but when they cannot imagine disobeying.*

There are, of course, counter-arguments worth considering. Some claim that invisible governance is less oppressive precisely because it avoids violence. Better to live in a society where exclusion from travel is the harshest penalty than one where dissent leads to execution. This perspective is not without merit; the decline of overt brutality is indeed a human achievement. Yet this view risks overlooking the deeper costs: when control is invisible, it is harder to resist, harder to even name. Citizens may not fear for their lives, but they may lose the unpredictability, creativity, and spontaneity that constitute genuine freedom. The absence of visible violence lulls societies into complacency, making them less vigilant about the gradual narrowing of autonomy. What is traded away is not survival, but the capacity for nonconformity.

The difficulty of mobilising resistance against invisible systems is compounded by their banality. Outrage is easier to sustain against images of brutality than against the quiet indignities of algorithmic exclusion. Few march in protest against a rating system; few risk arrest to oppose a change in platform design. Even whistleblowers who reveal the inner workings of surveillance systems struggle to ignite lasting movements. Edward Snowden's disclosures shook the world, yet within a few years, mass surveillance had not only persisted but expanded, integrated into the infrastructures of everyday life. Outrage dissipates when repression has no spectacle, when injustice is embedded in routines that feel too ordinary to fight. Invisible control is not only efficient; it is resilient.

The implications of obedience without violence extend beyond politics into culture and psychology. If systems of control no longer rely on overt repression, then concepts like resistance, protest, and rebellion must be reimagined. Traditional forms of dissent—marches, strikes, acts of defiance—are ill-suited to confronting invisible architectures. To resist, one must first perceive the control, and that perception is systematically obscured. The challenge is not only to act against oppression but to *see* the oppression in systems that present themselves as neutral, technical, or inevitable. This demands a new literacy of power, an ability to read design, data, and infrastructure as political tools.

At its core, the argument is stark: violence has become unnecessary because control has become more intimate. It works not on bodies but on choices, not through punishment but through design, not by threatening death but by shaping life. This is what makes resistance harder to mobilise. People are less likely to fight against systems they do not recognise as oppressive, especially when those systems deliver convenience, efficiency, and rewards. The danger is not that we will live under tyranny in the traditional sense, but that we will live under obedience so total, so embedded, that it feels indistinguishable from freedom.

Chapter 2

Freedom's Mirage

Freedom has long been the organising myth of modern societies. It is invoked in constitutions, enshrined in declarations, celebrated in markets, and defended in courts. To be free is to choose—where to live, what to say, what to buy, whom to love, how to vote. Choice, in its abundance, is presented as proof of autonomy. Yet in the digital age, where much of life is mediated through platforms, the meaning of choice is being quietly redefined. Clicking, posting, purchasing, and swiping feel like acts of self-determination, yet the options from which we choose have already been filtered, ranked, and framed by algorithms. The individual believes they are exercising agency, but the horizon of possible actions has been pre-structured in ways they rarely perceive. What appears as freedom increasingly reveals itself as design: a mirage shimmering with the promise of autonomy, even as it leads us down paths laid out by unseen hands.

This illusion is most evident in the architecture of digital platforms. A user scrolling through a newsfeed may feel empowered to select what content to engage with, but the feed itself is the result of algorithmic curation designed to maximise attention. Posts that align with prior behaviour rise to the surface; dissenting or unfamiliar perspectives are buried. The very perception of abundance masks a narrowing of genuine options. Search engines offer millions of results, yet the vast majority of users never look beyond the first page, where ranking systems quietly define relevance. E-commerce platforms present thousands of products, yet their recommendation engines funnel consumers toward a smaller subset, optimised not for user autonomy but for profitability and engagement. *Choice, in this context, is not eliminated but engineered.* The marketplace of options appears infinite, but its architecture channels behaviour in predictable and profitable directions.

The most seductive mechanism for sustaining this illusion is convenience. Modern societies are built on the acceleration of life: faster communication, faster transport, faster consumption. Platforms exploit this by offering frictionless services that save time, smooth transactions, and eliminate obstacles. One-click purchasing on Amazon or seamless payments through WeChat Pay feel liberating, removing the drudgery of effort. Yet this convenience comes at a cost: it locks users into ecosystems from which exit becomes increasingly impractical. Amazon Prime's promise of free delivery encourages loyalty while crowding out smaller competitors. WeChat Pay integrates chat, commerce, and banking into a single platform, making disengagement feel tantamount to self-exile from modern life. Like the Roman bread-and-circus model, these conveniences pacify by satisfying immediate needs while subtly conditioning compliance. Citizens come to accept the infrastructure that organises their lives, not because they are coerced, but because the alternative feels unbearably inconvenient.

The psychological shift from consent to conditioning lies at the heart of this transformation. Traditional social contracts were framed around explicit agreements: citizens consented to laws, workers to contracts, consumers to purchases. In the digital environment, however, consent has become less meaningful. Few users read terms and conditions; even fewer understand how their data will be used. Agreement is often secured through fatigue or indifference. More insidiously, once engaged, users are steered through design choices that cultivate habits. Notifications trigger responses, defaults encourage passive acceptance, and gamified features reward repetitive behaviours. Over time, the line between voluntary participation and conditioned obedience blurs. A user no longer consciously consents each time they unlock their phone or check their email; they are habituated into routines that platforms have carefully designed. *Obedience ceases to be an act and becomes a disposition.*

Perhaps the most deceptive dimension of this conditioning is the promise of personalisation. In theory, tailored recommendations enhance relevance, sparing individuals the noise of irrelevant information. In practice, they construct silos that confine individuals within predictive systems. A personalised newsfeed reduces exposure to unfamiliar viewpoints, reinforcing confirmation biases. A personalised shopping experience nudges consumers toward predictable purchases, discouraging exploration. A personalised social platform filters friendships, creating networks of sameness that shrink horizons of empathy. What feels like bespoke service is in fact a narrowing of possibility, where algorithms anticipate desires and shape futures on the basis of past behaviour. Agency becomes retroactive: individuals believe they are choosing, but their choices were predicted, channelled, and often predetermined. *The tyranny of personalisation lies in its subtlety: it limits freedom while presenting itself as its highest expression.*

The consequences of this shift are not confined to individual experiences; they reshape societies. Political discourse is increasingly mediated by platforms that filter content for engagement, amplifying outrage and polarisation. Economic opportunities are structured by algorithmic rankings that determine visibility and relevance, often without transparency. Cultural consumption is organised by recommendation engines that privilege popular or profitable content, reducing diversity and experimentation. The appearance of abundance conceals a consolidation of power, where a few platforms dictate the conditions of choice for billions. Resistance is difficult to mobilise because there is little overt repression to protest. Instead, citizens willingly trade autonomy for convenience, mistaking their compliance for empowerment.

The central theme of this chapter is therefore unsettling: freedom in the digital age often masks its opposite. The ability to click, buy, or post does not guarantee autonomy when the architecture of choice is pre-structured by invisible systems. Convenience seduces individuals into trading control for ease. Consent collapses into conditioning as habits are engineered by design. Personalisation narrows rather than expands the horizon of possibility. Together, these mechanisms create a mirage: the feeling of freedom without its substance. Recognising this requires a shift in perception, a willingness to interrogate not only the choices we make but the systems that make our choices for us. Only then can we begin to distinguish between genuine autonomy and its carefully crafted illusion.

When Choice Is Engineered

The hallmark of modern liberal societies is the belief that freedom is expressed through choice. To buy, to click, to post, to swipe—these actions are celebrated as demonstrations of individual agency. Yet the reality of digital life complicates this assumption. The menu from which we choose is rarely neutral; it has been pre-structured, ranked, and filtered long before we exercise our apparent freedom. What looks like autonomy is often a carefully engineered process in which algorithms, data models, and design features quietly decide what options reach us. *The illusion of choice is not the absence of alternatives, but the manipulation of which alternatives we see and how we see them.*

Consider the architecture of online search. Typing a query into Google may return millions of results, giving the impression of near-limitless possibility. But most users rarely go beyond the first few links. The order in which those links appear is determined by an algorithm designed to maximise relevance, profitability, and engagement—criteria invisible to the user. The choice presented is already curated, the horizon of possible knowledge subtly shaped. Similarly, on platforms like Amazon, customers browsing products are steered toward recommendations based on prior behaviour, trending items, or sponsored placements. A consumer feels they are selecting freely from thousands of goods, yet their attention has been channelled toward a narrow set of possibilities. The exercise of choice is genuine, but the field of available options has been invisibly constrained.

The mechanics of this engineering are not malicious by necessity; they emerge from the logic of digital platforms. Algorithms are built to reduce complexity, offering users the most "relevant" results. Yet relevance is never neutral. It reflects decisions about what counts as valuable, trustworthy, or profitable. Social media platforms curate feeds not to maximise diversity of thought but to maximise time spent on the platform. This means emotionally charged content is more likely to appear, while nuanced or unfamiliar material is buried. What looks like the open marketplace of ideas is in fact a system optimised for engagement. *The design of the menu is as important as the act of choosing from it.*

The illusion of abundance is particularly effective because it masks the narrowness of actual selection. Netflix, for example, boasts vast libraries of content, yet the overwhelming majority of users watch only what appears in their personalised recommendation rows. The appearance of freedom is sustained by the presence of choice, even if the paths of attention are guided by predictive models. In this sense, engineered choice differs from overt restriction. Unlike censorship, which removes options outright, engineered choice allows abundance to remain visible while nudging behaviour toward predetermined outcomes. This distinction makes resistance harder: it is difficult to protest against a narrowing of autonomy when the menu appears endless.

Engineered choice thrives on predictability. The more data platforms collect, the better they can anticipate what users are likely to select. Amazon predicts purchases, Spotify predicts songs, TikTok predicts entertainment preferences with uncanny accuracy. Each correct prediction reinforces user trust, deepening reliance on the system. But this predictability has costs. By feeding individuals what they are most likely to engage with, platforms reinforce past behaviours and limit exposure to the unexpected. The self is mirrored back, narrowing horizons under the guise of relevance. What feels like personalisation is often confinement. *The individual becomes legible to the system at the price of becoming less unpredictable to themselves.*

The consequences extend beyond consumption into political and social life. The "filter bubble" effect describes how algorithmic curation of news feeds exposes individuals primarily to perspectives that confirm existing beliefs. This is not merely a by-product of digital design but an engineered feature of engagement-driven algorithms. Outrage, confirmation, and repetition generate more clicks than ambiguity or challenge. The freedom to encounter diverse perspectives diminishes, even as the illusion of choice expands. Citizens feel informed because they scroll, click, and react—but the landscape of information they navigate has been carefully sculpted. Political opinions harden, not because citizens have chosen isolation, but because engineered choice has corralled them into echo chambers.

It is important, however, not to oversimplify. Engineered choice does not mean individuals are puppets without agency. People can resist, seek alternatives, or consciously expand their horizons. Yet the power of invisible design lies in its ability to shape defaults. Most users do not actively contest the ranking of search results, the curation of feeds, or the convenience of recommendations. Defaults become destiny because effort is required to escape them, and the pace of digital life discourages such effort. As behavioural economists note, individuals overwhelmingly stick with default options, whether in pension schemes, software settings, or online interfaces. *The subtle structuring of choice is often more decisive than the range of choices themselves.*

The philosophical implications of engineered choice challenge traditional understandings of freedom. If autonomy requires not only the ability to choose but meaningful diversity in what can be chosen, then algorithmic curation undermines the substance of freedom while preserving its appearance. A society in which people can click endlessly but rarely encounter uncurated possibility risks mistaking abundance for autonomy. The question is not whether people are free to choose, but whether the structure of choices presented preserves the conditions for genuine agency.

The engineering of choice also alters the relationship between individuals and institutions. In traditional governance, citizens could debate laws, challenge restrictions, or protest decrees. In algorithmic governance, the structuring of choice is often opaque, hidden in proprietary code and corporate secrecy. A consumer denied a loan due to an algorithmic decision has little recourse to contest the design of the scoring system. A content creator whose posts are buried by a platform's recommendation algorithm cannot appeal to a visible censor. Power operates not through visible command but through invisible design. The locus of contestation shifts from law and politics to infrastructure and code—domains shielded from public accountability.

What makes engineered choice so resilient is that it feels like freedom. The act of selecting, clicking, or swiping provides a constant reinforcement of agency, even as the parameters of those actions are pre-determined. The very repetition of choice sustains the illusion. Individuals believe they are shaping their lives, when in reality their lives are being shaped by systems designed to anticipate, guide, and monetise their behaviour. The challenge for modern societies is not simply to demand more choices, but to interrogate who structures those choices, how they are ranked, and what forms of agency they encourage or suppress.

To recognise when choice is engineered is to glimpse the subtle architecture of digital power. It does not deny individuals their capacity to act, but it channels that capacity into predictable pathways. The danger is not that freedom disappears, but that it becomes indistinguishable from conformity. The illusion of choice is maintained because the act of choosing remains; what is concealed is the narrowing of what is possible. This is the mirage of digital freedom: a horizon filled with abundance that leads, time and again, to the same engineered destinations.

Convenience as a Currency of Compliance

Modern societies are governed less by the threat of punishment than by the promise of ease. Where once states and empires secured loyalty through spectacle, ritual, and force, today obedience is cultivated through infrastructures of convenience so seamless that submission feels voluntary. The citizen does not bow to a sovereign; they subscribe to Amazon Prime. They do not queue for rations in the square; they order groceries delivered to their doorstep with a tap. The most potent forms of governance in the digital age are not the ones that restrict choice outright but those that make a particular choice so effortless that resistance becomes irrational. *Convenience has become the new currency of compliance, binding populations more tightly than fear ever could.*

The parallel to ancient pacification strategies is instructive. The Roman practice of *panem et circenses*—bread and circuses—was not about eliminating dissent through terror, but about dulling it through gratification. Citizens were distracted and satiated, their political energies redirected into consumption and spectacle. The logic persists in contemporary form, but instead of bread and entertainment, the modern citizen is pacified by free next-day delivery, streaming libraries, and frictionless digital payments. Amazon Prime guarantees abundance and speed; WeChat Pay offers the integration of chat, commerce, and credit into a single interface. These services appear as gifts of modernity, but they also function as infrastructures of dependence. Once embedded in everyday routines, their absence feels like deprivation, their withdrawal like punishment. *What pacification once achieved with food and games, modern platforms achieve with convenience and speed.*

The brilliance of convenience is that it masks control as service. The consumer frames their dependence as empowerment: "I can have anything delivered instantly," "I can pay without cash or card," "I can access endless entertainment on demand." Yet this empowerment is bounded by the architecture of the platform itself. Amazon shapes what products are visible, which sellers thrive, and how prices are set. WeChat Pay mediates not only transactions but also the flow of data, tying financial behaviour to a broader ecosystem of surveillance and state oversight. The user experiences efficiency; the system harvests compliance. In this trade, autonomy is surrendered not under duress but under the seduction of ease. *The less friction in a system, the more invisible the surrender it demands.*

This trade-off is not accidental; it is engineered. Frictionless design is a deliberate strategy to habituate users into dependence. Consider the "one-click purchase" patented by Amazon: by eliminating even the pause of entering a password or confirming an order, it accelerates impulse and reduces the likelihood of reconsideration. Consumers feel liberated from delay, but in practice they are being channelled into behaviours that maximise platform profit. Similarly, WeChat Pay integrates payments with communication, social networking, and government services, creating an ecosystem so comprehensive that opting out becomes socially and economically costly. What begins as convenience becomes necessity. Compliance emerges not because people fear punishment, but because life outside the system becomes unthinkable.

The political implications are profound. Traditional governance relied on visible authority: the tax collector, the guard, the official decree. Digital governance works differently. By embedding services into daily life, it ensures compliance without confrontation. When governments partner with platforms to integrate services—tax payments, identity verification, or health codes—the citizen's willingness to comply is secured not by compulsion but by the need to participate in basic functions of society. During the COVID-19 pandemic, for example, digital health codes in China, embedded into apps like Alipay and WeChat, determined who could travel, enter buildings, or access services. Compliance was near total, not because police patrolled every street, but because non-compliance meant exclusion from daily life. The infrastructure itself ensured obedience.

This logic extends beyond authoritarian contexts. In liberal democracies, loyalty to platforms is cultivated through perks and privileges that create habits of reliance. Amazon Prime users shape their shopping around the promise of rapid delivery, even when cheaper alternatives exist elsewhere. Netflix subscribers curate their cultural consumption within a platform that privileges its own productions. Apple Pay habituates consumers to a closed ecosystem of devices and services. These conveniences accumulate into structures of dependency that resemble governance, even if framed as commerce. *To govern through convenience is to bind citizens not with chains, but with habits they willingly adopt and rarely abandon.*

Yet convenience as governance raises unsettling questions about freedom. If autonomy is defined as the capacity to choose otherwise, then infrastructures that make opting out prohibitively costly erode that autonomy even without coercion. A user may technically be free to shop outside Amazon, to live without WeChat, or to forgo Prime and Pay. But the social, economic, and temporal costs of doing so are so great that the freedom becomes illusory. A city where everyone uses WeChat Pay punishes the cash-only holdout not through law but through exclusion from transactions. A society where rapid delivery and subscription services are the norm makes slower alternatives feel impractical, even irresponsible. The citizen is not forced, yet they comply. *Convenience narrows the field of viable options until submission feels like choice.*

Critics may argue that convenience is a neutral good, a sign of progress that saves time and expands access. Indeed, it would be a mistake to portray it as mere deception. The efficiencies of digital platforms are real; they improve lives, create opportunities, and reduce burdens. The issue is not that convenience itself is sinister, but that it is deployed as a governing logic without transparency or accountability. When convenience becomes the principal means of structuring compliance, it shifts the balance of power from citizens to systems that decide what forms of ease are available and under what conditions. Bread and circuses satisfied immediate needs but silenced political ones; modern convenience may satisfy personal desires while eroding collective capacities for resistance and reflection.

The currency of compliance, then, is not fear but habit. Individuals come to define their expectations of life through infrastructures of convenience, and in doing so, they normalise the trade of autonomy for speed, privacy for frictionless service, and choice for curated efficiency. What makes this trade so resilient is that it rarely feels like loss. It feels like progress. The queues are shorter, the payments faster, the deliveries quicker. Only on reflection does the paradox emerge: the more convenient life becomes, the more deeply individuals are bound to systems that shape their behaviour in advance. The citizen is pacified not because they are coerced, but because they are comfortable. And in the long history of governance, few currencies have been more stable than comfort.

From Consent to Conditioning

For centuries, the legitimacy of authority has hinged on the idea of consent. From social contract theory to democratic elections, societies have built their claims to legitimacy on the principle that people choose to be governed, whether through explicit agreement or tacit acceptance. In the digital age, however, this principle is undergoing a subtle but profound transformation. Consent, once understood as an active decision, is increasingly reduced to a perfunctory click, a box ticked, a set of unread terms and conditions scrolled past. Beyond this superficial ritual, platforms and systems have developed mechanisms that bypass choice altogether, cultivating habits and routines that steer behaviour without the need for renewed agreement. *The shift is from conscious consent to unconscious conditioning: from voluntary affirmation to obedience so deeply embedded that users no longer recognise it as compliance.*

The decline of meaningful consent is most visible in the ubiquity of digital contracts. Each time a person installs an app, subscribes to a service, or purchases online, they are asked to "agree" to a document few ever read. The legal fiction is that individuals freely enter these agreements, yet the reality is one of fatigue and inevitability. Opting out of consent is rarely feasible when participation in modern life requires engagement with platforms that dominate communication, commerce, and finance. In practice, users "agree" not out of deliberation but out of necessity, their agency reduced to a binary choice: participate or abstain. This is not the exercise of consent in any substantive sense but a ritualised surrender to systems whose terms are non-negotiable. Consent here is little more than a veneer of legitimacy.

Yet the more significant shift occurs after the initial agreement, when conditioning takes over. Platforms are designed not simply to capture consent once but to shape behaviour continuously. Notifications prompt immediate attention, nudging users into rhythms of checking and responding. Default settings exploit inertia, ensuring most users stick with the path chosen for them. Rewards—whether likes, discounts, or loyalty points—reinforce repetitive behaviours until they become habits. Over time, the act of choosing disappears. A person does not consciously decide each time they check their phone upon waking; they are conditioned into the act. A consumer does not weigh up alternatives when they reorder from the same platform; the routine has been ingrained. *Where consent demands awareness, conditioning thrives on automaticity.*

The psychological mechanics of this shift draw on decades of research into habit formation and behavioural economics. B.F. Skinner's experiments in operant conditioning demonstrated how animals could be trained to repeat behaviours when reinforced with rewards or deterred by punishments. Today's platforms apply these insights at scale, delivering variable rewards that maximise engagement. The unpredictability of notifications or recommendations mirrors the psychology of slot machines, keeping users hooked by the anticipation of novelty. Once such routines are established, they no longer require deliberate choice. Users respond reflexively, mistaking conditioned behaviour for preference. This distinction matters: *a habit repeated without reflection is not an expression of freedom, even if it feels self-chosen.*

Consider how social media platforms manage attention. The user consents, once, to join by creating an account. From then on, design takes over. Infinite scroll removes natural stopping points, encouraging prolonged engagement. Notifications are batched or timed to maximise return visits. The dopamine spikes from likes and comments reinforce posting behaviour. Over time, users log in not because they actively choose to, but because their attention has been trained to seek the stimulus. Consent has been replaced by conditioning. What began as voluntary participation becomes habitual obedience to platform rhythms.

E-commerce offers another case in point. A consumer consents to shop online by creating an account. Conditioning then transforms their behaviour. One-click purchasing reduces deliberation, loyalty schemes reward repeated use, and personalised recommendations narrow the scope of exploration. Before long, consumers reorder automatically, not because they have compared alternatives but because the system has trained them to associate speed and ease with satisfaction. The initial consent fades into irrelevance; the conditioning remains. The marketplace appears free, but its users are being steered into predictable patterns that prioritise platform dominance over genuine autonomy.

The implications for democratic legitimacy are striking. If traditional consent was the cornerstone of governance, what does it mean when conditioning takes its place? Citizens who no longer actively agree to surveillance but live comfortably within its architectures cannot be said to have consented meaningfully. A health app that tracks movement may rely on an initial click-through agreement, but its real power lies in conditioning users to accept monitoring as natural. A credit system that rewards punctual repayment and penalises default conditions behaviour far more effectively than any contract signed at the outset. The appearance of voluntary participation conceals a deeper truth: obedience has been cultivated, not consented to.

There are those who argue that conditioning is simply another word for culture or routine, that societies have always relied on the normalisation of behaviour rather than constant reaffirmation of consent. There is some truth in this. Schools, workplaces, and religious institutions have long conditioned individuals into patterns of obedience. Yet digital conditioning differs in two critical ways. First, it operates at a scale and speed unprecedented in history, with algorithms processing behavioural data in real time to refine nudges. Second, it is largely invisible, embedded in design rather than explicit instruction. Traditional conditioning was mediated by authority figures—teachers, bosses, priests—whose demands could be recognised and resisted. Digital conditioning is hidden in interfaces and defaults, making it harder to perceive, let alone contest.

The ethical tension lies in the erosion of awareness. Consent presupposes recognition: one must know what one is agreeing to. Conditioning bypasses this recognition, embedding obedience in routines that feel natural. This raises the uncomfortable possibility that many of the freedoms modern societies claim to preserve are illusory. A person who feels free because they can choose among apps, products, or platforms may in fact be exercising choices so conditioned that their autonomy is hollowed out. The individual does not feel coerced, yet their behaviour aligns precisely with the goals of the system. *Obedience without awareness is not freedom, even if it feels effortless.*

Recognising this shift matters because resistance requires awareness. One cannot resist conditioning one does not perceive. Citizens may rally against overt repression, but they rarely mobilise against the erosion of autonomy disguised as convenience. The political genius of conditioning lies in its subtlety: it produces obedience without triggering resistance. It is not that individuals lack agency altogether, but that their agency is continually steered, narrowed, and normalised until the act of questioning itself feels unnecessary. Consent was once the language of legitimacy; conditioning has become the architecture of control. The shift is not theoretical—it is lived daily, in the habits of billions whose behaviours align seamlessly with the interests of systems they no longer consciously choose to obey.

The Tyranny of Personalization

Personalisation presents itself as the hallmark of digital progress: a world tailored to each individual, where services anticipate needs, platforms curate relevance, and every interaction feels uniquely designed. The promise is seductive. Instead of being overwhelmed by endless options, individuals are guided to the most suitable choices. Newsfeeds are customised to reflect one's interests, playlists built to match one's mood, shopping recommendations fine-tuned to one's tastes. It appears to be a triumph of user empowerment. Yet beneath the sheen of relevance lies a profound shift in agency. *Personalisation, far from liberating, increasingly functions as a form of constraint, narrowing horizons of thought, preference, and action until autonomy is indistinguishable from prediction.*

The mechanics of personalisation rely on predictive systems that learn from past behaviour. Every click, search, and swipe feeds into an algorithm that refines its model of the user. The more one interacts, the more precise the predictions become. Spotify suggests songs based on prior listening, Netflix queues films similar to those already watched, Amazon recommends products aligned with previous purchases. The system grows adept at pre-empting desire, and in doing so, subtly reshapes it. What is presented as a personal preference is often an algorithmic suggestion that has become indistinguishable from one's own will. The line between choosing and being chosen for blurs. *When every recommendation feels natural, few stop to question whether they are directing their desires or being directed by them.*

One of the most striking consequences of personalisation is its tendency to lock individuals into feedback loops. An algorithm that learns a user's political leanings will prioritise news articles that reinforce those views, steadily filtering out dissenting perspectives. A shopping platform that notices repeated purchases in a particular category will double down on suggesting more of the same, discouraging exploration outside the established pattern. Social media feeds surface content that maximises engagement, often by intensifying existing preferences or emotions. Over time, the system does not merely reflect one's tastes; it actively shapes them, pushing individuals further into narrowed corridors of predictability. The breadth of possible experience is reduced, yet the narrowing goes unnoticed because it is experienced as comfortingly relevant.

This narrowing of agency under the guise of empowerment is what makes personalisation tyrannical. Tyranny need not announce itself with overt repression; it can emerge in systems that structure behaviour so effectively that alternatives fade into invisibility. A personalised newsfeed does not forbid individuals from accessing other sources, but it ensures they are less likely to encounter them. A personalised shopping experience does not prevent consumers from exploring independent vendors, but it makes the default path the curated marketplace of the platform. A personalised playlist does not ban access to unfamiliar genres, but it gradually erodes curiosity by presenting comfort as the optimal choice. *Freedom of choice exists in principle, but the personalised infrastructure makes deviation so unlikely that it becomes meaningless in practice.*

The psychological impact of this shift is profound. Humans are creatures of habit, and when systems consistently meet expectations, they encourage passivity. Individuals learn to outsource the labour of searching, comparing, and deciding to algorithms that appear efficient and accurate. The result is a form of cognitive dependency. Trust in algorithmic recommendations deepens because they rarely disappoint, yet that trust blinds users to the narrowing of their horizons. What feels like liberation from effort is in fact an erosion of critical faculties. The less one interrogates how choices are structured, the more one accepts them as natural. *Personalisation does not merely predict preference; it conditions it.*

The political implications are equally troubling. When citizens receive news and information through personalised feeds, their exposure to public life is mediated by algorithms optimised for engagement rather than deliberation. This has been linked to increased polarisation, as individuals are shown content that confirms biases and provokes emotional reactions. The public sphere, once imagined as a space of shared discourse, fragments into personalised silos where citizens inhabit distinct informational realities. Elections, referenda, and public debates are increasingly shaped by these algorithmic architectures, raising the question of whether democratic choice retains its substance when citizens are channelled into predictable patterns of belief and behaviour. The tyranny here is subtle: individuals feel informed, even empowered, but the breadth and diversity of their exposure is determined by systems that prioritise profit and influence over civic agency.

It would be misleading, however, to suggest that personalisation is wholly negative. For many, it offers genuine value: less time wasted searching, more relevant content, improved accessibility. In fields like healthcare, personalisation can mean earlier diagnoses, tailored treatments, and more efficient resource allocation. In education, it can support differentiated learning, adapting to students' strengths and weaknesses. These applications demonstrate that personalisation, when deployed responsibly, can enhance autonomy by supporting better decisions. The problem arises when personalisation becomes the default mode of interaction across all domains, eroding the capacity for serendipity, unpredictability, and independent choice. *When every encounter is curated, the possibility of the unexpected—the very essence of freedom—diminishes.*

The central question, then, is not whether personalisation is beneficial, but under whose terms it is governed. At present, personalisation is primarily driven by corporate imperatives: to capture attention, maximise engagement, and monetise data. Its architecture is shaped less by what serves the user than by what benefits the platform. This is why the tyranny of personalisation feels inescapable: it is embedded not as an optional service but as the underlying logic of digital life. Opting out requires significant effort and often entails exclusion from the efficiencies others take for granted. To resist is to slow down in a world that rewards speed, to accept inconvenience in a culture that prizes ease. Few are willing to pay this cost, and so compliance is secured not by coercion but by comfort.

The tyranny of personalisation lies in its success. It delivers relevance so efficiently that individuals rarely feel deprived, even as their agency is hollowed out. It shapes behaviour not by denying freedom but by making the predictable path the easiest one to follow. It confines not through prohibition but through abundance so carefully curated that alternatives wither from neglect. This is why it is among the most powerful forms of digital control: it leaves individuals feeling free while ensuring they act in ways that serve the system. To live under the tyranny of personalisation is not to be visibly oppressed but to be subtly guided until freedom itself becomes indistinguishable from conformity.

Chapter 3

The Algorithmic Eye

Surveillance has always been about watching, but watching has never been the endpoint of power. The gaze of monarchs, police, and intelligence agencies was historically directed toward detection—who was plotting, who was stealing, who was rebelling. Observation produced files, archives, and evidence. Today, however, surveillance has shifted its axis. It is no longer content with describing the past or documenting the present; it is oriented toward the future. The defining quality of digital surveillance is prediction. Modern systems are not designed merely to see what people are doing but to forecast what they will do next, and to act upon those forecasts in real time. The camera has become an oracle. The file has become an algorithmic model. The gaze does not only detect crime; it seeks to pre-empt it. In doing so, it transforms the very logic of control: from reactive discipline to anticipatory governance. *The algorithmic eye is not content to observe—it seeks to script the future before it arrives.*

This predictive turn is most visible in law enforcement. Across cities in the United States and the United Kingdom, predictive policing tools have been deployed that claim to identify neighbourhoods or individuals at heightened risk of criminal activity. These systems digest vast datasets—past arrests, reported crimes, demographic profiles—and output "hotspots" for patrols or names for monitoring. The rationale is efficiency: limited police resources can be targeted where they are most needed. Yet the results often expose a darker reality. Because the input data reflects historical patterns of policing, the outputs reproduce those same biases, disproportionately targeting marginalised communities already under scrutiny. Crime is not merely predicted; it is produced, reinforced by the very act of surveillance. A neighbourhood once designated a "risk zone" becomes subject to heightened patrols, ensuring more arrests, which then justify the designation anew. *The algorithm does not discover criminality; it manufactures it by amplifying existing inequalities.*

The danger here is not only statistical but philosophical. When individuals are treated according to predictions rather than actions, the presumption of innocence is quietly eroded. Citizens are judged not by what they have done but by what they might do, as inferred by a system whose logic is opaque. The science-fiction comparison to *Minority Report* is tempting, but the reality is less cinematic and more insidious. There are no clairvoyant "precogs," only data models that mistake correlation for causation, patterns for inevitability. Yet the consequences are real: heightened surveillance, increased stop-and-search, restrictions on mobility, all justified by probabilities. What was once the domain of fiction has become policy. The algorithmic eye does not simply watch; it condemns in advance.

But predictive surveillance extends far beyond policing. Corporations, too, have perfected the art of forecasting behaviour, though their goal is profit rather than justice. Tech giants like Google, Amazon, and Facebook rely on predictive analytics to anticipate consumer desires with uncanny accuracy. By analysing browsing histories, purchase patterns, and location data, they build behavioural profiles that allow them to predict, with high probability, what an individual will buy, click, or watch next. This predictive capacity is not ancillary to their business model—it is the business model. Advertising revenue depends not on broadcasting to the masses but on targeting individuals at precisely the moment they are most susceptible. In this sense, corporate surveillance economies operate on the same principle as predictive policing: identifying probable futures and acting to shape them. The marketplace of attention becomes governed by the same logic of anticipatory control.

What makes these predictive economies particularly potent is their alignment with state interests. Governments increasingly turn to corporate datasets to supplement their own surveillance capacities, blurring the boundaries between public authority and private enterprise. During the COVID-19 pandemic, for example, mobility data from tech companies was used to track compliance with lockdowns and predict potential outbreaks. In China, the integration of financial data from platforms like Alipay into state-run systems created a feedback loop between corporate convenience and government oversight. Even in liberal democracies, partnerships between law enforcement and technology firms have proliferated, with private platforms supplying data for security and intelligence purposes. The distinction between market-driven prediction and state-driven prediction becomes less meaningful when both rely on the same infrastructures of data extraction. *The algorithmic eye belongs to no single actor; it is a shared architecture of anticipatory power.*

The deeper transformation wrought by predictive systems lies in their redefinition of discipline. Traditional discipline punished deviance after it occurred, reinforcing norms by penalising violations. Predictive systems invert this logic. They discipline in advance by rewarding conformity and punishing unpredictability. Credit scoring systems, for instance, do not merely record financial histories; they shape future behaviour by making access to loans conditional on adherence to expected patterns. Health insurers use predictive analytics to reward lifestyle choices deemed low risk, subtly nudging clients into behaviours aligned with actuarial models. Employers monitor digital activity to forecast productivity, rewarding employees who conform to expected patterns of output and penalising those who deviate. *The accumulation of data creates a regime where unpredictability itself becomes a liability.* To be free is to be risky; to be predictable is to be rewarded.

The consequences for human agency are profound. When systems reward conformity and penalise deviation, individuals learn to internalise the logic of predictability. They moderate their speech online to avoid being flagged, tailor their financial behaviour to optimise their credit score, and shape their social interactions to preserve their ratings. Over time, these adjustments cease to feel like impositions. They become the fabric of everyday life. The algorithmic eye does not need to coerce; it only needs to make the costs of deviation high enough that compliance feels natural. Resistance becomes irrational, not because it is illegal but because it is inefficient, inconvenient, or costly. In this way, predictive systems succeed where brute surveillance often failed: they cultivate obedience not through fear but through the rational calculus of self-interest.

What emerges is a new form of governance, one that operates across the boundaries of state and market, law and commerce. It is anticipatory rather than reactive, probabilistic rather than deterministic, invisible rather than spectacular. Its hallmark is not the spectacle of punishment but the quiet calibration of incentives. Citizens are not dragged before courts; they are nudged by algorithms. Consumers are not forced to buy; they are presented with offers they find irresistible. Workers are not coerced to produce; they are monitored until self-discipline becomes second nature. The algorithmic eye oversees all of this, not with malice but with metrics. It does not watch in order to know; it watches in order to shape. And in that shaping, the line between prediction and prescription disappears.

This chapter examines the rise of the algorithmic eye in all its dimensions: its expansion beyond surveillance into prediction, its use in policing that mirrors science fiction yet entrenches social inequality, its role in corporate economies that monetise foresight, and its transformation of data into a tool of discipline that punishes unpredictability and rewards conformity. The central question it poses is not simply how much is being watched, but how deeply the future is being written in advance by systems that claim only to observe. To live under the gaze of the algorithmic eye is to live in a world where the future itself has become an object of governance, managed not by force but by probability, not by decree but by design.

Beyond Surveillance: Into Prediction

The act of watching has always been a form of power, but its limitations are obvious. Surveillance, in its traditional sense, produces knowledge of what is happening now or what has happened before; it identifies culprits, documents actions, and archives events. It is backward-looking and reactive, a tool of detection more than prevention. What distinguishes the digital era is the transition from watching to forecasting, from surveillance to prediction. The focus is no longer on merely recording behaviour but on anticipating it—and crucially, intervening before it occurs. This shift from retrospective control to anticipatory governance marks one of the most profound transformations in the logic of authority. *The surveillance state of the twenty-first century does not simply observe reality; it attempts to script it in advance.*

Predictive technologies emerge from the confluence of vast data accumulation and machine learning. Every search query, purchase, biometric record, GPS coordinate, and digital interaction feeds into models that seek patterns. Unlike earlier forms of monitoring, which required human interpretation, these models operate autonomously, generating probabilities about future behaviour. The significance of this development cannot be overstated: systems now claim to know not only what people have done, but what they are likely to do. Policing, healthcare, finance, marketing, and even education are increasingly mediated by such predictions. The implications are immense, for once behaviour is anticipated, interventions can be justified not on the basis of actual wrongdoing but on the probability of risk. *The very definition of deviance shifts from what has happened to what might happen.*

Few domains illustrate this shift as starkly as policing. In cities across the United States, predictive policing tools such as PredPol and CompStat claim to identify "hotspots" of likely crime. Patrols are then dispatched pre-emptively to those areas, in effect treating probabilities as certainties. The result is a self-fulfilling cycle: neighbourhoods flagged as risky receive disproportionate police attention, leading to higher arrest rates, which then reinforce the dataset that justifies further policing. The communities caught in this loop are overwhelmingly poor and often racially marginalised. A predictive model, built on historical data, inherits historical prejudice. It does not predict crime in any objective sense; it predicts where police are likely to look. In the United Kingdom, similar systems have been trialled to assess individuals considered at risk of future offending, raising profound questions about due process and civil liberties. When prediction stands in for evidence, suspicion becomes indistinguishable from guilt.

The predictive turn also alters the state's approach to political life. Systems that monitor social media do not simply catalogue dissent; they forecast protest movements and unrest. Governments can pre-emptively disrupt gatherings, detain organisers, or flood zones with security forces before a march begins. The mere possibility of dissent becomes sufficient justification for intervention. This is no longer the traditional logic of surveillance, which sought to detect opposition in order to respond, but a more insidious logic of prediction, in which opposition is neutralised before it can manifest. The chilling effect is intensified: not only does one risk punishment for what one has done, but one may also face intervention for what one has not yet done, on the basis of probabilities assigned by a machine.

Corporate actors have perfected predictive systems for different ends, though the mechanics are strikingly similar. Tech giants monetise foresight by predicting consumer behaviour. Google anticipates what a user will search before they finish typing. Amazon predicts purchases and positions warehouses accordingly. Netflix predicts what viewers will watch and commissions content based on aggregate forecasts of demand. The aim is efficiency and profit, but the implications echo those of predictive policing. When platforms shape offerings based on anticipated desires, they not only predict behaviour but influence it. A consumer shown a curated set of options is more likely to choose from within that set, reinforcing the model's accuracy. Over time, desire itself becomes shaped by what the system predicts. *The predictive model does not merely reflect preference; it produces it.*

The boundary between corporate prediction and state prediction is increasingly porous. Governments draw on corporate datasets to enhance their forecasting, while corporations benefit from regulatory environments that encourage or mandate predictive analytics. During the pandemic, predictive models of mobility and infection patterns were fed by location data from mobile phones, supplied by telecom providers and app developers. Health codes, which determined access to public spaces in countries like China, were based not only on actual test results but on predictive risk scores. Even in democracies, insurance companies and employers are experimenting with predictive health analytics, using wearable data to forecast future illness and incentivise particular behaviours. The predictive state and the predictive market converge on a shared logic: shaping conduct by forecasting it.

What distinguishes prediction from surveillance is its normative force. Surveillance reveals what has already happened; prediction assigns risk to what has not yet occurred. In doing so, it creates categories of suspicion that blur the line between possibility and inevitability. The person flagged as a future offender, the neighbourhood marked as a hotspot, the protest labelled as a potential riot—all are subject to pre-emptive intervention. The problem is not merely that predictions can be wrong, though they often are, but that they restructure social life around probabilities. To be risky is to be treated as guilty; to be unpredictable is to be treated as dangerous. *The algorithmic eye rewards conformity not because it is virtuous, but because it is predictable.*

The philosophical stakes are significant. Prediction raises the question of free will in a new and urgent form. If human behaviour can be forecast with high accuracy, what happens to the idea of autonomy? More importantly, when institutions act on these forecasts, autonomy is not only philosophically undermined but practically constrained. Individuals are nudged, rewarded, penalised, or excluded based on what they are likely to do. Their futures are partially written before they act. In this way, prediction becomes a form of governance. It disciplines not by punishing transgression but by making transgression improbable in the first place. People adjust behaviour pre-emptively, not to avoid punishment after the fact but to avoid risk scores, exclusion, or loss of privilege before anything has happened. Control is achieved not by coercion but by foresight operationalised as constraint.

The transition from surveillance to prediction thus marks a watershed in the history of power. Where surveillance catalogued, prediction scripts. Where surveillance responded, prediction anticipates. Where surveillance documented deviance, prediction disciplines deviation before it occurs.

To live under predictive systems is to inhabit a world where the future is no longer open but probabilistically managed. The paradox is that this management is often invisible. Citizens and consumers rarely perceive predictive interventions as control; they experience them as safety, convenience, or relevance. Yet beneath the appearance of service lies a deeper logic of governance, one that reduces autonomy to a variable in a model and freedom to a probability score. The act of watching has evolved into the act of forecasting—and in that shift, the balance of power tilts decisively from those being observed to the systems that claim to know their future.

Predictive Policing and Minority Report Realities

When police departments in Los Angeles first began trialling predictive policing tools, the promise was deceptively simple: algorithms would identify areas most at risk of crime, allowing officers to deploy resources more efficiently. The initiative was marketed as a rational, data-driven upgrade to policing, free from human bias and grounded in statistical objectivity. Yet the reality soon became apparent. Neighbourhoods already heavily policed, often poorer and more ethnically diverse, were repeatedly flagged as "high risk," justifying even greater scrutiny. Officers returned, more arrests were made, and the data fed back into the system, confirming the algorithm's initial prediction. What emerged was not a neutral assessment of crime risk but a self-reinforcing cycle of surveillance and control. *Far from eradicating bias, predictive policing has automated and entrenched it, turning historical inequalities into future certainties.*

The phrase "Minority Report policing" is often used to describe these systems, invoking the dystopian vision of citizens arrested for crimes they have not yet committed. The comparison is apt in one sense, but misleading in another. There are no clairvoyant "precogs" foreseeing future murders, only algorithms working with incomplete, noisy, and biased datasets. Yet the consequences are similar: individuals and communities treated as threats not because of what they have done, but because of what they might do. In Chicago, a controversial programme known as the "Strategic Subject List" sought to identify individuals most likely to be involved in shootings, either as victims or perpetrators. Thousands of names appeared on the list, many with no serious criminal record. The effect was not preventive justice but heightened surveillance and suspicion for those flagged by opaque criteria. The logic of prediction blurred into pre-emptive punishment.

In the United Kingdom, experiments with predictive policing followed a similar trajectory. The Durham Constabulary trialled an algorithmic system called Harm Assessment Risk Tool (HART), designed to predict the likelihood of reoffending among suspects. Those deemed high risk faced stricter bail conditions or monitoring. Proponents hailed the tool as a pragmatic way to allocate limited resources. Critics pointed out that the system was trained on historical arrest data, which inevitably reflected existing patterns of over-policing in disadvantaged areas. This meant that individuals from poorer postcodes, or with certain demographic profiles, were statistically more likely to be categorised as high risk. The system thus translated social inequality into algorithmic destiny. *The pretence of objectivity masked the reality that predictive tools were not forecasting the future so much as amplifying the past.*

Defenders of predictive policing argue that data-driven methods are still preferable to subjective human judgment, which is demonstrably prone to prejudice. They contend that algorithms can be audited, improved, and standardised in ways that individual decision-making cannot. There is merit to this claim, yet it overlooks a central truth: when the data itself is biased, the system is structurally incapable of fairness. In the United States, decades of discriminatory policing practices—stop-and-frisk policies, disproportionate arrests for drug offences, racially skewed sentencing—have created datasets that overrepresent minority communities as criminal. Feeding this history into predictive tools ensures that those same communities will remain under perpetual suspicion. What appears as technological neutrality is, in practice, the mechanisation of systemic injustice.

The problem is compounded by opacity. Many predictive systems are proprietary, developed by private firms that guard their algorithms as trade secrets. This creates a black box effect: citizens cannot know how risk scores are calculated, nor challenge their categorisation. In Los Angeles, the predictive policing programme PredPol was eventually abandoned after widespread criticism that its operations were opaque, unaccountable, and discriminatory. Yet by then, its logic had already diffused to other jurisdictions. The issue is not confined to one tool or one city; it reflects a broader trend in governance, where authority is ceded to algorithmic systems whose workings remain hidden from public scrutiny. *When the rationale for intervention is concealed within proprietary code, accountability evaporates.*

The consequences are not limited to immediate policing outcomes. Predictive systems reshape the relationship between citizens and the state, eroding the principle of equal protection under the law. Communities targeted as "high risk" live under conditions of heightened surveillance, with knock-on effects for education, employment, and mobility. Employers may be reluctant to hire individuals from areas stigmatised as crime hotspots. Landlords may shy away from renting to those associated with predictive risk categories. A probabilistic designation, once applied, follows individuals in ways that are socially and economically debilitating. The effect is cumulative: predictive policing not only directs law enforcement but also stratifies opportunities, embedding inequality into the very fabric of daily life.

The inevitability of predictive policing, however, must also be acknowledged. The allure of efficiency, the promise of prevention, and the availability of data make it highly attractive to overstretched police departments and governments eager to demonstrate innovation. In an age where resources are scarce and political pressure for safety is constant, predictive tools appear to offer a rational solution. They fit neatly within a broader culture of algorithmic governance, where sectors from finance to healthcare are turning to predictive analytics as the gold standard of decision-making. To reject predictive policing outright may seem, to policymakers, like clinging to outdated methods. *The danger lies in this very inevitability: once normalised, predictive systems become part of the unquestioned infrastructure of governance.*

Yet inevitability does not mean desirability. Recognising the risks of predictive policing requires a clear-eyed understanding of its limitations. Algorithms cannot eliminate bias when the data itself is biased. Predictions cannot establish guilt or intent, yet they are increasingly treated as justification for intervention. The language of efficiency obscures the human costs: the communities subjected to intensified surveillance, the erosion of due process, the chilling effect of being deemed risky without recourse. At stake is more than the fairness of policing. What predictive policing reveals is a deeper shift in how societies understand justice itself: from the adjudication of actions to the management of probabilities. In this transformation, the very foundations of legal and political legitimacy are at risk.

Predictive policing may present itself as a tool of safety, but its consequences are corrosive. By embedding historical bias into future governance, it perpetuates injustice under the guise of progress. By acting on probabilities, it undermines the principle that individuals should be judged for what they have done, not what they might do. And by cloaking its logic in technical neutrality, it shields itself from accountability. The "Minority Report" comparison is not a fanciful exaggeration but a warning. The danger is not that machines will foresee the future with perfect clarity, but that societies will accept imperfect predictions as sufficient grounds to curtail freedom. The algorithmic gaze, once adopted, is difficult to resist. It promises efficiency but delivers inequality. It promises foresight but entrenches prejudice. And in doing so, it quietly transforms the very meaning of justice from a right to be defended into a probability to be managed.

Corporate Surveillance Economies

When Google first declared that its mission was to "organise the world's information," it presented itself as a public utility of knowledge, a service designed to democratise access. What it did not emphasise was that the real commodity was not information itself but the ability to anticipate and shape human behaviour. Every search query, location ping, and browsing trail fed into models that could predict what users might want next. These predictions became the foundation of a vast advertising empire that today generates hundreds of billions of dollars annually. This pattern—collecting data, generating predictive insights, and monetising influence—has since become the organising principle of the corporate surveillance economy. *The world's most powerful companies are not merely intermediaries of communication or commerce; they are architects of behavioural futures, where profit is secured by forecasting and nudging human action.*

Unlike traditional forms of commerce, where goods or services were sold in exchange for money, the surveillance economy operates on a subtler transaction: users trade data for access, convenience, or entertainment. What appears free—search engines, social networks, navigation apps—is underwritten by the capture of personal information. That information is processed into predictive models that can forecast what a person will click, buy, or believe. Advertisers then purchase access to these predictive outputs, ensuring their messages appear at the moment of maximum susceptibility. The product is not the software itself but the probability of a user's future behaviour. In this sense, *personal data is not merely harvested; it is transformed into a raw material for behavioural prediction, which is then packaged and sold as a market commodity.*

The implications extend well beyond advertising. Platforms such as Facebook (now Meta) and TikTok have demonstrated how predictive analytics can be used to maximise attention itself. By modelling engagement patterns, these platforms deliver personalised content designed to keep users scrolling for longer. The longer the scroll, the more data is generated; the more data, the more precise the predictions; the more precise the predictions, the more valuable the system to advertisers. This feedback loop has been described as surveillance capitalism's engine: the commodification of not just what people say or do, but how they spend their time and what captures their gaze. Attention becomes both the resource extracted and the product sold. *The predictive economy thrives on habit formation, ensuring that platforms are not just services used but environments inhabited.*

The corporate surveillance economy does not operate in isolation. Its predictive capacities align seamlessly with the goals of state power, particularly in the domains of security and governance. Governments, facing challenges from terrorism, cybercrime, and political dissent, find corporate datasets invaluable. Partnerships between technology companies and law enforcement agencies have proliferated, often with little public oversight. Google's subsidiary, Sidewalk Labs, pitched "smart city" projects where urban infrastructure would collect real-time behavioural data, ostensibly to optimise efficiency but also to create opportunities for surveillance integration. Amazon's Ring doorbell cameras have been linked with police departments across the United States, creating neighbourhood-wide surveillance networks that blur the boundary between private property and public policing. These collaborations illustrate how corporate predictive analytics not only serve market goals but also become tools of governance. *Profit and control are not opposing forces but mutually reinforcing logics within the surveillance economy.*

The symbiosis between corporations and states is particularly visible in contexts of crisis. During the COVID-19 pandemic, technology firms provided predictive mobility data to governments seeking to manage lockdowns and anticipate outbreaks. Apple and Google jointly developed exposure notification systems that tracked proximity between devices, enabling large-scale public health monitoring. While justified as emergency measures, these tools normalised the use of corporate predictive infrastructure for state purposes. Once developed, such systems rarely disappear; they are repurposed for security, commerce, or political control. The pandemic thus accelerated a convergence already underway: predictive analytics as the connective tissue linking corporate profit with state governance.

The consequences of this convergence are profound for individual autonomy. In the corporate domain, predictive analytics nudge consumers toward purchases, habits, and content that maximise profitability. In the state domain, predictive analytics identify risks, threats, and deviance before they manifest, enabling pre-emptive intervention. Together, these systems create an environment where behaviour is continuously managed, not through explicit coercion but through probabilities and incentives. To deviate from predicted patterns is to risk exclusion: lower credit scores, fewer job opportunities, increased surveillance. To conform is to be rewarded with convenience, relevance, and access. *The logic of the corporate surveillance economy thus aligns seamlessly with the logic of governance: both thrive by reducing uncertainty, disciplining unpredictability, and normalising conformity.*

Critics often suggest that greater transparency or consumer choice could mitigate these dynamics, but the structure of the surveillance economy undermines such solutions. Opting out of data collection is rarely feasible without withdrawing from essential services altogether. Few can realistically abandon email, search engines, or messaging platforms. Even those who try find themselves captured through indirect means, as their friends, families, and colleagues generate relational data that implicates them. Moreover, predictive analytics operate at a scale where individual consent becomes meaningless. The value lies in aggregated patterns, not isolated choices. As a result, the economy functions less as a marketplace of voluntary exchange than as an infrastructure of inevitability. Users participate not because they choose to but because non-participation is practically impossible. *Surveillance capitalism is not a sector of the economy but its hidden operating system.*

The alignment of market goals with state control mechanisms raises a critical question: who governs the governors? If predictive analytics are shaping the behaviour of billions, and if corporations wield them in ways that serve both profit and state power, accountability becomes a vanishing point. Regulatory efforts, such as the European Union's General Data Protection Regulation (GDPR), have sought to curb the most egregious forms of data exploitation, but enforcement lags behind technological innovation. Meanwhile, companies adapt quickly, finding new ways to extract predictive value within legal grey zones. States themselves, reliant on corporate datasets, have little incentive to impose strict limits. The very institutions tasked with protecting citizens from surveillance economies are often complicit in sustaining them.

The corporate surveillance economy is not simply a commercial system; it is a mode of governance in its own right. By monetising prediction, tech giants have created infrastructures that align profit with control, convenience with compliance, personalisation with conformity. What began as a business model has become a political force, shaping not only what individuals buy or watch but how societies define freedom, risk, and responsibility. The predictive economy thrives by making the future calculable, but in doing so it constrains the openness of that future. *The price of convenience is not merely data; it is the gradual surrender of unpredictability, the very condition of human freedom.*

Data as the New Discipline

A society saturated with data is not simply one that observes more—it is one that governs differently. The accumulation of information on human behaviour, once justified as a means of documentation or efficiency, has become a mechanism of discipline in its own right. What is striking is that mass data collection does not remain a neutral record of reality. It intervenes in reality, subtly and persistently, by rewarding those who conform to established patterns and penalising those who deviate. The line between surveillance and governance blurs until the act of being measured is indistinguishable from the act of being controlled. *In a data-driven world, obedience is not demanded through violence or decrees, but induced through the quiet compulsion of metrics.*

Consider the example of credit scoring. Originally designed to assess the financial risk of lending, the credit score has evolved into a proxy for trustworthiness itself. A high score unlocks cheaper loans, rental agreements, and even employment opportunities, while a low score can relegate individuals to economic precarity. What matters here is not whether a person has committed a crime or broken a rule, but whether their data patterns signal predictability and reliability. Paying bills on time, maintaining stable debt ratios, avoiding sudden financial moves—all of these become signs of conformity rewarded with access and privilege. Conversely, unpredictability—missing a payment, switching jobs too frequently, or engaging in erratic spending—becomes grounds for exclusion. The score disciplines individuals into regularity. It teaches that stability, even when personally constraining, is the safest path to social and economic acceptance.

This logic extends beyond finance. Ride-sharing platforms such as Uber and food delivery apps like DoorDash deploy rating systems that bind workers and customers alike to regimes of conformity. Drivers and couriers know that a few low ratings can jeopardise their ability to earn; passengers are aware that poor behaviour risks refusal of service. What emerges is a reciprocal discipline mediated by data. Neither party may face overt punishment by the state, yet both adjust behaviour pre-emptively to maintain favourable scores. The system operates as an invisible regulator: compliance becomes not only rational but instinctive. *Metrics turn reputation into a quantifiable form of power, exerting control not through law but through the ever-present possibility of exclusion.*

In workplaces, employee monitoring software has become increasingly pervasive, tracking keystrokes, mouse activity, or time spent on specific applications. Companies justify these measures as ensuring productivity, but their effect is more profound: they transform the rhythms of daily labour into datasets that reward conformity to an ideal worker profile. Employees learn to minimise breaks, optimise task completion times, and avoid behaviours that might register as inefficiency. The dataset becomes the arbiter of performance, often more decisive than a human manager. Workers, aware of constant observation, discipline themselves to fit the data profile demanded of them. Here again, unpredictability—pauses in activity, irregular schedules, deviations from output norms—is treated not as creativity or individuality but as a liability. The workplace thus becomes less a site of negotiated effort and more a laboratory of quantifiable compliance.

The disciplinary nature of data becomes clearest when unpredictability is not only discouraged but actively penalised. Predictive policing, for instance, relies on past data to forecast future crime. Neighbourhoods deemed "high risk" receive disproportionate police attention, often resulting in higher arrest rates that feed back into the dataset. Residents in these areas are disciplined not because of their individual actions but because the collective data marks them as risky. The very act of living in an unpredictable environment becomes grounds for suspicion. This is not discipline in the classical sense—punishment after transgression—but discipline in a new sense: constant pressure to minimise variance from the norm. *When the data itself determines risk, deviation becomes a crime in waiting.*

The power of data lies in its ability to redefine normality. Historically, norms were established through cultural traditions, legal codes, or moral consensus. Today, norms are increasingly statistical. What is common, average, or predictable is coded as safe; what is rare, irregular, or surprising is coded as risky. This shift has profound consequences for freedom. Freedom often expresses itself in unpredictability—the sudden career change, the unexpected protest, the unconventional lifestyle. Yet in a system that disciplines through data, unpredictability is punished with lower scores, greater scrutiny, or exclusion from benefits. The cost of freedom rises in proportion to the value placed on conformity. Individuals internalise this cost and gradually adjust behaviour, trading spontaneity for stability, creativity for consistency, divergence for compliance.

It is tempting to imagine that individuals can simply opt out of these systems, but in practice withdrawal is nearly impossible. Credit scores, rating systems, predictive algorithms, and monitoring infrastructures have become embedded in the fabric of everyday life. To forgo participation is to lose access to housing, employment, mobility, or social trust. Moreover, even if one refuses to generate data directly, relational data—friends, colleagues, family connections—ensures that one remains implicated in the network. Opting out is not an escape but a different form of exclusion. Thus, the system disciplines not only through participation but through the impossibility of avoiding participation. *The universality of data ensures the universality of discipline.*

Some defenders of data-driven governance argue that these systems increase fairness and transparency, replacing subjective judgment with objective metrics. There is some truth here: credit scores may eliminate certain forms of discriminatory lending; performance data may reveal inefficiencies overlooked by managers. Yet the deeper issue is that metrics, however precise, redefine what counts as fairness itself. To be predictable becomes synonymous with being trustworthy; to deviate becomes synonymous with being irresponsible. The metric does not simply measure fairness—it constructs it. In doing so, it shifts the moral landscape of society, where conformity is rewarded not because it is virtuous but because it is legible to the system.

The rise of data as discipline also demands a rethinking of power. Michel Foucault described the shift from sovereign power, which punished the body, to disciplinary power, which trained behaviour. What we witness now is a further evolution: *algorithmic power*, which disciplines not through direct commands but through the probabilistic shaping of possibility. It does not forbid in the traditional sense but renders some actions costly and others effortless. It nudges individuals away from unpredictability by attaching risks to it, while smoothing the path for conformity. The result is a society where deviation is not outlawed but economically, socially, and politically disincentivised. Discipline is no longer visible in the lash or the prison cell; it is hidden in the credit score, the rating, the algorithmic filter.

The consequences of this transformation are subtle yet pervasive. People learn to edit themselves before the system does, to pre-emptively align with what is expected, to reduce variance in their digital and physical lives. The constant awareness of being measured produces a form of anticipatory compliance that seeps into decision-making at every level. Should I post this comment online, knowing it may affect future employment? Should I take a financial risk, knowing it may lower my credit score? Should I act unpredictably, knowing the system values conformity? The very act of questioning reveals the presence of discipline: the metric already governs by shaping the horizon of what feels possible.

Data has become the new discipline not because it punishes more harshly but because it punishes more subtly. Its genius lies in its invisibility, in the way it makes compliance feel like choice and conformity feel like common sense. It recasts unpredictability not as a space of freedom but as a liability to be avoided. In doing so, it reshapes human conduct, not with chains or decrees but with probabilities, scores, and incentives. The future it envisions is one where freedom is measured in data points, where conformity is the price of participation, and where unpredictability—the essence of human agency—becomes the rarest and riskiest act of all.

Chapter 4

Obedience by Design

Power today is not exercised only through laws or punishments, nor even through the raw accumulation of data. It is increasingly embedded in the very design of the systems that structure daily life. The digital interfaces we touch, the metrics that evaluate our performance, and the devices that track our habits are not passive tools—they are architectures that shape behaviour with quiet precision. Rather than demanding obedience, they elicit it by making compliance the easiest, most natural, and often most rewarding path. What is striking is that this design does not merely reflect human psychology; it exploits it. Subtle prompts, defaults, and feedback loops transform free choices into predictable behaviours. The effect is not overt coercion but a patterned conformity that arises because systems are designed to guide us into it. *Obedience today is less an act of submission than the outcome of interacting with environments that have been engineered for compliance.*

Behavioural economics provides one of the clearest illustrations of this process. When policymakers or corporations discovered that small tweaks to choice architecture—such as making organ donation the default option—could dramatically increase compliance, they found a method of governance that avoided confrontation altogether. These "nudges" function not by forbidding alternatives but by making one option overwhelmingly more convenient or likely. Digital platforms have taken this principle and scaled it to billions. Default privacy settings on social networks often lean toward maximum data sharing, requiring effort and awareness to change. Subscription services make cancellation a maze while sign-up is effortless. The lesson is consistent: people overwhelmingly accept the path of least resistance. By building systems that embed certain defaults, designers ensure mass compliance without needing to issue commands. *The most powerful rules are the ones that appear as neutral design choices rather than explicit directives.*

Beyond nudges, the gamification of everyday life represents a more explicit harnessing of psychological reward systems. The structure of points, ratings, and badges, familiar from video games, now permeates education, fitness, shopping, and work. Fitness apps celebrate daily streaks; ride-hailing drivers are evaluated through ratings; employees compete on productivity dashboards. These systems tap into deep-seated human tendencies for competition, recognition, and reward. Yet while the mechanics feel playful, their function is disciplinary. They train individuals to chase metrics, often at the expense of intrinsic motivation. A driver may adjust behaviour not because of professional standards or personal ethics, but because a low rating threatens income. A worker may prioritise easily quantifiable tasks over creative or long-term contributions because only the former register on the dashboard. In this sense, gamification transforms obedience into a game where winning means conforming to the system's metrics. *The addiction lies not in entertainment but in the continual drive to align oneself with the algorithm's expectations.*

What makes this discipline particularly effective is its normalisation through everyday exposure. Children raised on classroom management apps or digital monitoring systems learn early that constant observation is ordinary. Students whose attendance, performance, and even emotional states are logged in real time grow accustomed to environments where data defines their identity. Employees onboarded into companies with monitoring software or productivity trackers quickly learn that surveillance is not an exception but part of workplace culture. These practices do not provoke resistance because they are framed as efficiency measures, safety tools, or methods of improvement. Over time, obedience ceases to feel like something imposed and instead feels like the natural way to participate in modern institutions. *When surveillance is woven into the routine of education, employment, and daily life, compliance becomes second nature.*

The domestication of surveillance through consumer devices further deepens this process. Consider the rise of products like Ring, Fitbit, and workplace dashboards. A Ring doorbell ostensibly provides security, but it also creates a localised surveillance system that can feed into broader networks, sometimes in collaboration with law enforcement. A Fitbit tracks fitness, but in doing so it trains users to evaluate health not by personal well-being but by data metrics, from step counts to sleep quality. Workplace dashboards, marketed as tools for transparency, condition employees to measure their worth through quantifiable performance indicators. These devices are willingly purchased and embraced by users, making them distinctive from state-imposed monitoring. Their appeal lies in the promise of empowerment—safety, health, productivity—but their effect is to establish habits of self-monitoring and external accountability. *The consumer becomes both the surveilled and the willing participant in their own disciplining.*

The common thread across these practices is that design has become the most effective medium of governance. By embedding expectations into defaults, rewards, and feedback loops, systems can shape behaviour without overt force. The result is obedience not experienced as oppression but as convenience, play, or normality. Individuals feel they are exercising choice, yet the architecture of those choices has been meticulously structured to guide them toward predictable, compliant outcomes. What makes this form of power difficult to resist is its subtlety. There is no obvious oppressor, no single law to protest, no visible punishment to oppose. Instead, there is a series of everyday interactions that feel trivial in isolation but cumulative in effect. To resist means not simply to reject a rule but to step outside entire infrastructures that organise modern life.

This chapter examines how obedience has been designed into the systems that now govern behaviour. From the psychology of nudges to the gamified pursuit of metrics, from the normalisation of surveillance in schools and workplaces to the consumer embrace of monitoring devices, the mechanisms of compliance are increasingly embedded in the environments we inhabit. What unites them is their reliance on design rather than decree, psychology rather than punishment, participation rather than repression. Understanding these mechanisms requires seeing design not as neutral but as political, not as technical but as behavioural governance. *Obedience today is not enforced by visible chains but cultivated through environments that make it feel like the natural, inevitable, even desirable way to live.*

The Psychology of Nudges

One of the most disquieting developments in modern governance and commerce is the discovery that people can be guided into compliance without ever feeling coerced. At the heart of this transformation lies the concept of the "nudge"—a subtle alteration in the architecture of choice that steers individuals towards particular decisions while maintaining the illusion of autonomy. The power of the nudge is not that it removes options but that it rearranges them in such a way that the majority of people will predictably gravitate towards the path desired by the designer. It is precisely this invisibility, this blending of persuasion and design, that makes nudges so potent. They operate in the blind spot of human decision-making, exploiting cognitive shortcuts, biases, and tendencies that most individuals neither recognise nor resist. *Nudges are the art of making obedience feel like choice.*

The intellectual foundation of nudging emerged from behavioural economics, a field that challenged the traditional view of humans as rational actors. Experiments consistently demonstrated that people are swayed by defaults, framing, and social cues far more than by cost-benefit analysis. If joining a pension scheme requires individuals to opt in, participation rates may languish around 30 per cent; if the default is reversed and individuals must opt out, participation can soar above 90 per cent. The difference lies not in law, compulsion, or persuasion but in the design of the form. This insight—that the ordering of choices determines outcomes—revolutionised not only public policy but also corporate strategy. Governments realised they could increase organ donation rates or vaccination uptake without new laws. Companies recognised they could shape consumer behaviour with interface tweaks and default subscriptions. The lesson was unmistakable: to control behaviour, one need not restrict it—one must simply design its context.

Nowhere is this clearer than in the digital world, where platforms engineer interfaces that funnel users towards profitable behaviours. Consider the ubiquitous "accept all cookies" button on websites. Technically, users have the freedom to reject intrusive data collection, but the rejection process is often buried in layers of menus and complex language, while acceptance requires a single click. Predictably, the overwhelming majority comply with surveillance practices they might otherwise object to. Similarly, social media platforms exploit defaults in notification settings, ensuring that users are bombarded with alerts unless they take the time and expertise to disable them. Few ever do. What emerges is a system where the apparent freedom to choose masks a deeper reality: the architecture is designed to make one choice almost inevitable. *Compliance becomes not the result of informed consent but of frictionless default.*

Nudges are not limited to technical interfaces; they also shape behaviour through environmental cues and social framing. Supermarkets place certain products at eye level to increase sales; cafeterias promote healthier diets by making fruit more accessible than sweets. In each case, the structure of the environment does the work of discipline. What distinguishes digital nudges from these older practices, however, is scale and precision. Online platforms do not rely on general heuristics but on real-time data about individual preferences. Algorithms test which arrangements of buttons, colours, or words yield the highest compliance, iterating until behaviour is predictably patterned. Whereas the supermarket shelf might nudge millions in the same way, digital platforms personalise nudges to each user. What feels like a neutral interface is, in fact, a finely tuned system designed to exploit that particular user's cognitive vulnerabilities. *The intimacy of data transforms nudging from a general technique into a personalised technology of control.*

Supporters of nudges often argue that they are benign, even beneficial. A government that nudges citizens into saving for retirement or eating healthily might be said to enhance well-being without restricting liberty. There is merit in this defence: nudges can reduce harm, correct for biases, and encourage socially beneficial behaviour. Yet the ethical tension arises from the asymmetry of power. When corporations deploy nudges, their purpose is rarely the flourishing of the individual; it is the maximisation of profit. When governments use nudges, the line between paternal care and paternalistic manipulation becomes perilously thin. The individual may retain the formal ability to resist, but in practice resistance requires awareness, effort, and expertise that few possess. Thus, the nudge transforms autonomy into a formal rather than substantive reality: freedom is technically available but practically foreclosed.

The insidious strength of nudges lies in how quickly they recede into invisibility. Once defaults and prompts are established, people stop perceiving them as interventions and instead accept them as part of the natural environment of choice. A generation raised on social media platforms may never question why algorithms decide what content appears in their feed. Consumers accustomed to automatic subscription renewals may stop noticing how much control they have ceded to default billing. Over time, nudges cease to feel like nudges at all. They become the background architecture of decision-making, invisible and unquestioned. This invisibility is precisely what makes them so effective as tools of obedience. *The less an individual notices being steered, the more effectively the steering takes hold.*

It is also worth recognising how nudges reframe the very idea of governance. Traditional law operates through explicit rules and visible sanctions: break the rule, face the punishment. Nudges, by contrast, govern behaviour through design rather than command, shaping outcomes not by forbidding alternatives but by making them less likely. This creates a form of governance that is harder to contest. Citizens can challenge laws, debate policies, or protest against punishments. But how does one protest a default setting? How does one resist a notification architecture designed to demand attention? By embedding governance into design, nudges shift power away from the public realm of debate into the private realm of technical configuration. Decisions about behaviour are not made in parliaments or courts but in design studios and algorithmic models, shielded from public scrutiny. *The politics of nudges lies not in their visibility but in their quiet removal from democratic contestation.*

Critics sometimes argue that the power of nudges is overstated, pointing out that individuals can and do resist. This is true, but it misses the point. The effectiveness of nudges does not depend on universal compliance but on predictable majority behaviour. If 80 per cent accept the default option, the system achieves its purpose. Moreover, the burden of resistance falls disproportionately on the most vigilant and resourceful individuals, reinforcing inequalities. Those with time, education, or technical knowledge can disable notifications, adjust settings, or opt out of manipulative defaults. Those without these resources are left to absorb the full force of behavioural design. The result is not only compliance but stratified compliance, where the disadvantaged are more likely to be steered and less likely to resist. Nudges thus reproduce existing social hierarchies even as they claim neutrality.

The implications of nudges extend beyond the individual to the collective. When millions of people are nudged in similar directions, entire patterns of social life shift. Voter turnout can be increased or decreased by altering the design of registration systems. Consumer demand can be channelled towards particular products or services, reshaping markets. Online discourse can be amplified or muted by the arrangement of feeds and notifications. At scale, nudges are no longer about personal decision-making but about the governance of populations. The boundary between persuasion and control becomes indistinguishable. *A society of nudged individuals is a society governed not by visible laws but by invisible architectures of choice.*

What makes nudges so central to the contemporary landscape of obedience is not merely their effectiveness but their seamlessness. They require no confrontation, no explicit coercion, no recognition of submission. They work because they align with human tendencies toward inertia, convenience, and cognitive shortcuts. In doing so, they reveal a new logic of power: to govern people, do not command them—design their environment so that the command is unnecessary. The psychology of nudges thus illuminates the broader theme of obedience without violence, showing how compliance can be engineered through design rather than demanded through decree. It is a form of governance that feels voluntary yet operates on the most involuntary aspects of human cognition. And it is precisely because it feels voluntary that it is so difficult to resist.

Gamified Control

Few mechanisms of modern behavioural governance are as deceptively powerful as gamification. The practice of turning everyday actions into games—complete with points, badges, rankings, and streaks—might appear trivial, even playful, but beneath its colourful interface lies a sophisticated system of behavioural conditioning. What was once confined to arcades and consoles has migrated into workplaces, schools, fitness apps, and even state governance. The principles are drawn from psychology as much as from entertainment design: to reward predictable behaviour, punish deviation subtly, and keep individuals striving towards outcomes that serve the interests of the system. *Gamification is not just about making tasks engaging; it is about converting obedience into a game, and in doing so, making it addictive.*

The essence of gamification lies in harnessing reward loops. Every notification of a completed task, every digital badge, every upward tick in a ranking provides a small surge of dopamine. This neurochemical reinforcement is the same mechanism that underlies gambling and slot machines, making each act of compliance feel like a victory. Yet the victory is hollow: it exists only within the parameters set by the system's designers. A fitness app congratulates a user for walking ten thousand steps, not because that number has inherent meaning, but because it is the metric the app has chosen to promote continued engagement. In this sense, gamified systems manufacture significance, converting arbitrary thresholds into objects of pursuit. *The point is not the badge itself but the training effect it generates—the transformation of voluntary action into habituated compliance.*

This approach is not confined to consumer applications. Workplaces increasingly employ gamification to monitor and drive employee performance. Call centre workers, for example, may see their productivity ranked on dashboards that display leader boards visible to the entire team. Top performers are celebrated with badges, while those at the bottom face public shame or implied reprimand. The structure mimics a game, but the stakes are real: career advancement, job security, or even basic dignity at work. By dressing surveillance in the language of competition, employers transform discipline into motivation. Workers strive not only to avoid punishment but to achieve symbolic rewards, often sacrificing autonomy in the process. The illusion of play conceals the intensification of control.

A striking dimension of gamification is its portability across cultural and political contexts. In China, the logic of gamification has been scaled into the Social Credit System, where citizens can earn or lose points based on behaviour ranging from bill payments to online speech. At its core, the system is a national scoreboard, ranking individuals according to their compliance with state-sanctioned norms. Yet even outside explicitly authoritarian contexts, similar logics are at play. Uber drivers live under a constant system of ratings, where passenger evaluations determine continued access to work. Airbnb hosts, YouTube creators, and even ordinary social media users are embedded in ecosystems where stars, likes, and shares function as currencies of reputation. What links these examples is the same behavioural principle: the transformation of complex human interactions into simplified scores that govern opportunity and status.

The brilliance of gamified control is that it requires little overt enforcement. When people are conditioned to monitor their own progress against external metrics, they become self-disciplining subjects. A smartwatch wearer feels guilty for missing a step goal, even though no law obliges them to walk. An employee anxiously checks their productivity dashboard, even without a manager's intervention. A driver takes extra care with passengers, not because of civic duty, but to preserve their five-star rating. The metrics function as invisible overseers, turning internal motivation into a conduit for external power. *By embedding control in systems of reward, gamification achieves what punishment rarely can: willing, even enthusiastic, submission.*

Yet the apparent neutrality of gamified systems demands scrutiny. Who decides which behaviours are rewarded? Who sets the thresholds for success? These decisions are not natural but political. When an education platform rewards students for logging in daily, it encourages ritual engagement rather than critical thinking. When an e-commerce site gives badges for frequent purchases, it promotes consumption rather than sustainability. When a workplace ranking system prizes speed of task completion, it may undermine quality or well-being. What is framed as objective measurement is in fact an ideological choice about what to value and what to neglect. Gamified systems therefore do not merely measure behaviour; they shape it according to the interests of their designers. *To play the game is to accept the rules, even when those rules are invisible.*

Critics have compared gamification to a digital panopticon—an environment where people behave as if they are constantly watched. But in some ways, gamified control is subtler and more effective. Rather than instilling fear of punishment, it instils desire for reward. Instead of suppressing behaviour through coercion, it channels energy towards system-defined goals. Unlike the prison guard, the badge does not need to threaten—it seduces. The result is a form of power that is both less visible and more totalising. It colonises leisure as well as labour, consumption as well as production, everyday life as well as professional life. The scoreboard becomes a portable prison, carried in one's pocket and checked voluntarily.

Supporters of gamification often argue that it improves engagement, promotes productivity, and makes mundane tasks enjoyable. There is truth to this claim. A fitness app can encourage healthier habits; a classroom game can motivate disengaged students; a recycling competition can boost participation in sustainability initiatives. But to stop at these benefits is to miss the deeper implications. When gamified structures pervade every domain of life, the very concept of motivation is transformed. People learn to act not for intrinsic reasons—health, knowledge, civic duty—but for extrinsic rewards defined by systems they did not design. Autonomy erodes, not through force, but through an economy of points and badges that feels natural, even entertaining. *The danger is not that gamification forces people to behave, but that it teaches them to stop asking why they are behaving at all.*

The addictive qualities of gamification also warrant attention. Like gambling, gamified systems thrive on intermittent reinforcement—rewarding users unpredictably to keep them engaged. Social media likes are perhaps the clearest example: one post may garner a flood of validation, the next almost none. The unpredictability keeps users returning, checking, and posting in pursuit of the next dopamine surge. This creates cycles of dependency where individuals feel compelled to play the game, even when it undermines their well-being. The structure is exploitative, designed not to maximise human flourishing but to maximise engagement metrics, advertising revenue, or productivity outputs. In this light, gamification is not simply a design choice; it is a business model.

At scale, gamified control reshapes culture itself. When reputations are quantified, people curate themselves for points rather than for authenticity. When workplaces gamify performance, collaboration may suffer as individuals compete for rankings. When governance adopts scoring systems, citizenship becomes transactional, measured in credits rather than in rights. These cultural shifts normalise obedience as play, eroding the boundary between voluntary participation and systemic discipline. The promise of gamification—that it makes life fun—is inseparable from its peril: that it trivialises control, making it palatable and pervasive.

The phenomenon of gamified control reveals much about the new face of power in the digital age. It shows how obedience can be engineered not by threats but by incentives, not by repression but by engagement. It demonstrates how systems can cultivate conformity by making non-conformity feel like losing a game no one wants to lose. And it underscores a central paradox: that in pursuing rewards, individuals may unwittingly surrender freedom. The badge, the ranking, the point—all seem harmless, even entertaining. Yet each is a step towards conditioning obedience through design. And once the game is everywhere, the question is no longer whether one chooses to play, but whether one can ever stop.

The Normalisation of Surveillance

The most effective forms of power are not those that shock the senses or command attention but those that sink quietly into the rhythms of everyday life, becoming so familiar that they pass without question. Surveillance today operates less as an extraordinary intrusion and more as a mundane condition of existence. Children encounter it in classrooms, employees confront it in workplaces, and citizens internalise it in public and private spaces. What was once an exception—the watchful eye of authority—has become a steady background hum, shaping expectations and habits so early and so persistently that obedience begins to feel like common sense rather than imposition. *The danger lies not in the shock of surveillance but in its normalisation, the way it weaves seamlessly into life until it seems natural, even necessary.*

Schools offer some of the clearest illustrations of how surveillance is naturalised from a young age. Once, discipline was mediated primarily through teachers' authority and peer dynamics. Today, digital technologies extend the reach of oversight far beyond the classroom. Proctoring software watches students take exams through their webcams, scanning for suspicious eye movements or background noise. Attendance can be recorded automatically by biometric scanners or geolocation tracking. Even homework submissions are monitored by plagiarism detection systems that compare every essay against global databases. While justified in the name of fairness, efficiency, or academic integrity, these practices subtly train students to accept constant evaluation as the baseline of learning.

To be educated is no longer simply to acquire knowledge but to perform under perpetual scrutiny. A generation grows up internalising the lesson that their intellectual worth is validated by systems that watch, score, and archive their every move.

This conditioning extends smoothly into the workplace. Modern office life is often structured around productivity dashboards, keystroke monitors, and activity trackers that record how employees spend their time. Remote work, rather than liberating workers from oversight, has intensified it through monitoring software that captures screenshots, logs mouse activity, and flags periods of inactivity. Logistics workers wear wristbands that track their movements across warehouses; delivery drivers are judged by GPS records of their routes and timing. Even in white-collar professions, project management tools and communication platforms quietly amass data on patterns of responsiveness, collaboration, and efficiency. The language of "optimisation" and "transparency" masks what is, in essence, a system of continuous behavioural assessment. The office becomes an echo of the classroom: performance is not only measured by output but policed through constant digital presence. *To work is to be watched, and to be watched is to work better—or at least, more predictably.*

Children and employees are not the only ones enrolled in this culture of constant oversight. In public life, surveillance cameras are so ubiquitous that their presence barely registers. Cities justify them as deterrents to crime, but they also cultivate habits of self-regulation. A pedestrian crossing a street lined with cameras may not consciously feel restricted, yet their behaviour is subtly guided by the knowledge of visibility. More invasive still are facial recognition systems, increasingly used in airports, shopping centres, and even schools, which convert fleeting appearances into permanent data points. These technologies collapse the distinction between private and public behaviour, teaching individuals that every movement might be captured, recorded, and analysed. Over time, the feeling of being watched is replaced by the assumption of being watched, a psychological shift that reshapes conduct in ways that are difficult to disentangle from genuine choice.

The normalisation of surveillance is reinforced by consumer technology that encourages self-monitoring as a desirable lifestyle practice. Fitness trackers like Fitbit and smartwatches monitor heart rates, sleep cycles, and step counts, turning personal health into a stream of quantifiable metrics. Home devices such as Amazon's Ring cameras allow individuals to monitor their own front doors but also create vast networks of neighbourhood surveillance, often shared with law enforcement. These tools are marketed as empowering, offering users greater control over their lives. Yet they also embed surveillance as self-care and community responsibility, blurring the line between voluntary tracking and coerced monitoring. *When surveillance becomes a tool of personal empowerment, its disciplinary character disappears from view, replaced by the language of progress and convenience.*

The long-term consequence of such practices is a generational shift in what counts as normal. Children who grow up under classroom cameras or parental monitoring apps do not regard surveillance as extraordinary but as an ordinary condition of safety and learning. Employees entering the workforce after years of digital schooling accept productivity dashboards as natural extensions of their educational environment. Citizens accustomed to being recorded in public spaces rarely challenge the proliferation of cameras, having never experienced a world without them. The cultural baseline shifts, narrowing the space for questioning whether surveillance should exist at all. Resistance becomes harder to mobilise not because surveillance is too powerful but because it feels too familiar. *The triumph of modern surveillance lies not in its force but in its banality.*

It is tempting to view these developments as the inevitable price of modernity, but the normalisation of surveillance is not a neutral process. It is shaped by specific decisions made by institutions, corporations, and governments about what to monitor, how to monitor, and for what purposes. Schools could foster trust and integrity without biometric attendance; workplaces could measure outcomes rather than micromanage activity; cities could prioritise community engagement over omnipresent cameras. The fact that surveillance has become the default option reflects a deeper cultural logic: a preference for control, efficiency, and predictability over freedom, spontaneity, and trust. Each new generation raised within this framework inherits not only the tools of surveillance but the assumptions that justify them. What once required explicit justification—"why should this be monitored?"—becomes a silent expectation: "why would it not be?"

There are, of course, moments of resistance. Students object to invasive proctoring software, citing privacy and equity concerns. Workers push back against intrusive productivity tracking, framing it as a violation of dignity. Citizens challenge the spread of facial recognition technologies in public spaces. Yet these instances remain fragmented, often drowned out by broader narratives of safety, fairness, or convenience. It is difficult to resist what has already been absorbed into the texture of daily life.

The normalisation of surveillance does not crush dissent; it erodes its plausibility by making oversight seem both harmless and inevitable.

The deeper question, then, is not simply whether surveillance exists but how its normalisation shapes our very sense of freedom. If obedience becomes naturalised—if children, students, and workers grow up expecting to be monitored—then autonomy risks being redefined as compliance within the boundaries of visibility. Freedom becomes the ability to move smoothly within systems of oversight rather than the capacity to act beyond them. This redefinition is subtle, often unnoticed, but profoundly consequential. It does not merely change how people behave; it changes what they believe freedom to be. And once freedom is reimagined as compatible with constant surveillance, the possibility of reclaiming a different kind of autonomy may vanish from the collective imagination.

Case Study: Ring, Fitbit, and Workplace Dashboards

The most insidious forms of control are those that disguise themselves as empowerment. Devices like Amazon's Ring doorbell, Fitbit fitness trackers, and the dashboards that structure modern workplaces were never marketed as tools of surveillance or obedience. On the contrary, they were introduced as enablers of convenience, security, productivity, and health. Yet beneath their promises lies a subtle training mechanism: they transform individuals into both the subjects and enforcers of monitoring, drawing people into cycles of self-regulation and external compliance. What unites them is not their technical architecture but their cultural effect. Each device recruits the user into a regime of visibility and data extraction, where compliance is not demanded with threats but cultivated through habit, reassurance, and perceived benefit. The story of these technologies is less about their novelty than about their role in shifting the boundary of what feels acceptable to watch, record, and measure.

Consider Ring, the video-enabled doorbell owned by Amazon. On the surface, it embodies the idea of community empowerment: homeowners can monitor their property, deter crime, and share footage with neighbours. Yet the network effects of Ring extend far beyond individual households. Partnerships with police departments in the United States, for example, have turned Ring into a distributed surveillance system, allowing law enforcement to access footage without traditional warrants. Citizens, in effect, become unpaid extensions of the state's security apparatus, normalising the idea that safety requires constant vigilance. This outsourcing of policing to ordinary households not only blurs the line between private and public security but also reshapes behaviour. Delivery drivers may alter their conduct knowing they are likely recorded at every doorstep; neighbours may become suspicious of one another, encouraged by Ring's accompanying app, *Neighbours*, which fosters a culture of constant alertness. What appears as a tool of empowerment also conditions communities to equate safety with perpetual monitoring, embedding surveillance into the very definition of responsible citizenship.

If Ring habituates communities to surveillance, Fitbit and other wearable trackers foster compliance at the level of the body itself. By quantifying steps, sleep, and heart rates, these devices promote the ideal of the self as a measurable project—one whose worth is reflected in numerical outputs. The rhetoric is one of motivation: feedback is immediate, progress is visible, and goals are gamified. Yet the underlying effect is disciplinary. Fitbit conditions individuals to monitor themselves relentlessly, framing well-being as adherence to quantified targets. The device does not shout commands; it vibrates gently to remind you to move, awards digital badges for milestones, and quietly compares your data against broader user trends. The consequence is a subtle shift in agency. Choices about rest, diet, or activity no longer emerge solely from embodied intuition but are mediated through algorithmic feedback loops. What once belonged to the private domain of self-care is now overseen by an ecosystem of sensors, data analysts, and insurers increasingly interested in using such information to predict and shape behaviour. *Self-tracking becomes self-disciplining, and autonomy is replaced by alignment with invisible metrics.*

Workplace dashboards extend these dynamics into the professional sphere, turning productivity into a visible, measurable, and competitive exercise. From project management platforms to sales-tracking dashboards, employees increasingly inhabit environments where their contributions are logged, visualised, and ranked. On the surface, these systems promise transparency and accountability. Managers can see at a glance who is ahead of schedule, while employees can benchmark their performance against peers. Yet the reality is more complex. Dashboards create a culture where workers are encouraged to optimise for what is measured, often at the expense of creativity, reflection, or collaboration. When every keystroke, email, or completed task becomes part of a scorecard, the incentive is to perform visibly rather than meaningfully. The result is not only heightened pressure but the internalisation of metrics as a form of self-governance. Employees learn to anticipate how their actions will appear in dashboards, shaping behaviour in advance of oversight. The mechanism of compliance lies not in the threat of reprimand but in the cultivation of anticipation: the sense that every action is already inscribed in a ledger that will eventually be read.

What ties these cases together is the way they transform individuals into both the objects and agents of monitoring. With Ring, homeowners volunteer to surveil themselves and their neighbours, believing it enhances security. With Fitbit, users willingly track their bodies, convinced it enhances health. With workplace dashboards, employees adapt to being measured, believing it enhances productivity. Each example reveals how surveillance no longer feels imposed but chosen, woven into everyday practices of responsibility, efficiency, and self-improvement. This choice, however, is structured by design. Ring is built to connect private monitoring with state policing; Fitbit is built to gamify compliance with health metrics; dashboards are built to reward visible activity. The architecture of these tools ensures that users participate in systems that extract data and enforce conformity, even as they experience them as beneficial. *The genius of modern surveillance is not that it coerces but that it recruits—making compliance feel like participation.*

There is also a deeper cultural consequence. These devices reframe values such as safety, health, and productivity through the lens of measurement. Safety becomes the absence of unseen activity outside one's door; health becomes the accumulation of steps or minutes of sleep; productivity becomes the completion of quantifiable tasks. In each case, qualitative aspects of life—trust in one's neighbourhood, the subjective experience of well-being, the creative process of work—are marginalised in favour of quantifiable proxies. The metrics come to dominate the reality they claim to represent. In doing so, they reduce complex human experiences to data points, privileging conformity to measurable norms over unpredictability or dissent. The cumulative effect is a narrowing of what it means to live well, be safe, or succeed. To deviate from the norm—whether by refusing to track, resisting to share, or working at a rhythm unsuited to dashboards—is to risk exclusion, suspicion, or failure.

Critically, these systems illustrate the convergence of personal choice and structural control. Nobody forces individuals to buy a Ring camera, strap on a Fitbit, or log into workplace dashboards. Yet declining to do so increasingly carries social, economic, or professional costs. A household without surveillance cameras may be seen as careless, an employee resistant to dashboards as uncooperative, an individual without a tracker as uninterested in self-improvement. Compliance becomes not only habitual but socially expected. *The illusion of choice masks the reality of obligation, as cultural norms and institutional pressures transform voluntary adoption into de facto requirement.* This is the logic of obedience without violence, where control operates less through prohibition than through the careful calibration of incentives and expectations.

What these cases ultimately reveal is that consumer devices are not neutral tools but training instruments. They teach individuals to monitor themselves and others, to equate compliance with responsibility, and to align their behaviour with the metrics that systems deem valuable. They render surveillance intimate, embedding it in the home, the body, and the workplace. And they normalise obedience by making it appear not as submission but as empowerment. The danger is not that people are forced to comply but that they no longer recognise compliance as such. In this subtle reconfiguration of daily life, the very meaning of autonomy is reshaped: freedom becomes the ability to perform well within monitored systems, not the capacity to exist beyond them.

Chapter 5

Cultural Complicity

When the conversation turns to surveillance, Western democracies often comfort themselves with a convenient illusion: the belief that intrusive monitoring is the defining feature of authoritarian regimes, a distant problem belonging to Beijing rather than Boston, Moscow rather than Manchester. Citizens in liberal societies are reassured by their ballots, their courts, their free press, and are quick to dismiss the possibility that the tools of control are quietly embedding themselves within their own infrastructures. Yet this distinction is increasingly fragile. Democracies, too, have embraced cultures of monitoring, not by openly coercing populations but by weaving surveillance into the fabric of everyday life under the banners of safety, efficiency, and progress. The blind spot is cultural rather than technical. It is not that Western states and corporations lack the capacity for pervasive oversight but that they frame its use in terms that feel protective, benevolent, even aspirational.

The language through which surveillance is normalised is rarely one of repression. It speaks instead of empowerment and collective good. Citizens are encouraged to see cameras not as watchtowers but as guardians against crime, algorithms not as censors but as curators of relevance, biometric systems not as shackles but as gateways to seamless convenience. Safety, innovation, and national pride become the vocabulary of compliance. The decision to scan a face, track a movement, or log a purchase is reinterpreted as an act of modern citizenship, a contribution to the greater good. This linguistic sleight of hand creates an environment in which resistance feels unreasonable, even irresponsible. Who would reject a technology that promises protection from terrorism, streamlined travel, or a more personalised service? The deeper question—what freedoms are reshaped or eroded in the process—tends to disappear beneath the glow of progress.

The parallels between East and West become clearer when one shifts from rhetoric to logic. In Beijing, the social credit system openly ties rewards and punishments to behaviour, constructing a digital scaffold of conformity. In Silicon Valley, the same behavioural principles are cloaked in consumer-friendly design. A low credit score may limit your access to housing; a low Uber rating may limit your access to rides. A public square blanketed with state-installed cameras may feel different from a retail space filled with private sensors, yet both environments rely on the same assumption: people can be guided more effectively by predictive feedback and visible metrics than by laws alone. The political systems differ, but the behavioural DNA is shared. Both depend on citizens internalising the idea that they are always visible and that deviation will carry consequences—social, financial, or legal.

The COVID-19 pandemic offered a striking demonstration of this convergence. Contact tracing apps and digital health passes, rolled out across continents, made surveillance appear not only acceptable but necessary. The urgency of protecting public health dissolved traditional scepticism, allowing even the most privacy-conscious societies to adopt tracking technologies without significant resistance. In countries like South Korea, where early and aggressive digital tracing helped contain outbreaks, citizens came to see surveillance as a patriotic duty. In Europe, governments framed health passes as temporary measures, yet their adoption normalised the expectation that entry to public life could be conditioned on data disclosure. In the United States, tech giants collaborated with public authorities to build tracing frameworks, embedding corporate infrastructure deeper into state functions. The pandemic did not invent digital surveillance; it accelerated its social legitimacy, recasting it as benevolent care rather than coercive control. *A generation that once hesitated at the idea of location tracking now accepted it as the cost of collective safety.*

What is crucial to recognise is that complicity is not imposed but cultivated. Democracies rarely demand obedience through force; they invite it through persuasion, by presenting surveillance as an ally in the pursuit of security, prosperity, and health. Citizens, in turn, adapt to these narratives, embracing the tools that promise protection while overlooking their longer-term implications. The cultural complicity lies in this tacit bargain: trading away unpredictability for reassurance, uncertainty for control. The surveillance cultures of the West do not look like those of authoritarian states because they do not need to. Their genius is in their subtlety, in the way they transform monitoring into something people voluntarily adopt, defend, and perpetuate.

This chapter examines how that complicity is sustained. It interrogates the blind spots that allow liberal societies to underestimate their own surveillance cultures, the seductive language that frames monitoring as progress, and the structural similarities that tie Western democracies and authoritarian states to the same behavioural logic. Through the lens of case studies such as COVID-19 contact tracing, it shows how surveillance crosses borders not simply as a technology but as a cultural pattern—one that citizens themselves help entrench. The argument is not that democracy has failed, but that its defences against overreach are weaker than assumed. The line between empowerment and control, between care and coercion, is far thinner than many would like to believe. By the end of this chapter, the reader is invited to confront an uncomfortable truth: the endurance of digital dictatorship does not rest solely on authoritarian states but also on the quiet, willing complicity of societies that imagine themselves free.

Western Liberalism's Blind Spot

Few things flatter the self-image of liberal democracies more than the assumption that surveillance is primarily the tool of authoritarian states. It is Beijing, not Berlin; Moscow, not Manchester; Pyongyang, not Paris, that is imagined as the natural habitat of mass monitoring. Citizens of liberal societies console themselves with the belief that democratic institutions, independent courts, and a free press form a bulwark against the overreach of surveillance. Yet this assumption—comforting though it may be—is profoundly misleading. The reality is that democracies are not exempt from surveillance cultures; they simply package and justify them differently. By treating authoritarian excesses as alien, Western societies have cultivated a dangerous blind spot: the inability, or unwillingness, to see the scale and depth of monitoring at home.

The irony is that many of the surveillance technologies most closely associated with authoritarian regimes were either developed in or refined by liberal democracies. Closed-circuit television, now synonymous with the British high street, was first tested in Germany during the 1940s and adopted across Western Europe decades before China scaled it to unprecedented levels. Data aggregation techniques that power state monitoring in China owe much to Western advances in behavioural marketing and predictive analytics. Yet Western narratives tend to position these same technologies as benign or consumer-friendly. A system that tracks citizens' movements in Beijing is authoritarian; a system that tracks consumers' clicks in New York is innovative. Both systems rely on the same logic: visibility and data produce control.

This blind spot is reinforced by cultural framing. In democracies, surveillance is often sold as protection rather than repression. Cameras on street corners are justified as deterrents against crime. Digital monitoring in workplaces is defended as a means of boosting productivity. Biometric checks at airports are introduced as mechanisms for efficiency and national security. At every point, the language of empowerment masks the underlying reality: the expansion of systems that capture, categorise, and constrain human behaviour. Citizens internalise these justifications to the extent that refusing surveillance feels irrational or antisocial. To decline facial recognition on a phone is not framed as defending privacy but as choosing inconvenience. *This reframing of surveillance as progress allows democracies to advance control without confronting their own contradictions.*

The case of the United States illustrates this clearly. For decades, Americans were warned of state overreach, with dystopian fiction and political rhetoric positioning government as the primary threat to freedom. Yet the most significant surveillance apparatus in the country today is not state-owned but corporate, with companies like Google, Facebook, and Amazon tracking individuals at a granularity most intelligence agencies could only dream of. These corporations package their intrusions as services—search results, social connectivity, personalised shopping—yet the by-product is the same: a population whose choices, preferences, and movements are continuously monitored. The liberal framework permits this by defining freedom in terms of consumer choice, even as those choices are engineered by the very platforms that profit from surveillance. The irony is stark: authoritarian states are accused of controlling their citizens, while democracies invite their citizens to pay for the privilege of being monitored.

Europe, often cast as a regulatory counterweight to American tech dominance, exhibits its own contradictions. The General Data Protection Regulation (GDPR) is heralded as a global gold standard for privacy protection. Yet the continent is also one of the most heavily surveilled regions on earth, with the United Kingdom alone operating millions of CCTV cameras and deploying sophisticated data-sharing systems across public and private sectors. GDPR may restrict how corporations store and use data, but it does little to limit the expansion of state surveillance in the name of counterterrorism or border security. The paradox is that privacy law and surveillance culture can grow simultaneously, creating a political environment where citizens feel protected while being more monitored than ever.

The Western blind spot is not just political but psychological. People in democracies are more willing to accept surveillance when it is voluntary, incremental, and tied to convenience. Signing up for a loyalty card, installing a smart doorbell, or wearing a fitness tracker rarely feels like submitting to a monitoring regime. Each decision is framed as individual choice. But aggregated, these decisions amount to something much larger: a cultural acceptance of constant oversight. The distinction between authoritarian and democratic surveillance thus becomes one of style rather than substance. Authoritarian regimes impose surveillance overtly; democracies invite citizens to adopt it willingly, often with enthusiasm. The outcome—a population habituated to monitoring—is strikingly similar.

This willingness to externalise the problem onto authoritarian states creates geopolitical consequences as well. Western governments routinely criticise China's surveillance practices, particularly the social credit system, as uniquely repressive. Yet the structural similarities to Western systems—credit scores, algorithmic rankings, predictive policing—are rarely acknowledged in public discourse. The critique serves a strategic function, reinforcing democratic identity by defining freedom against an authoritarian other. But it also obscures the fact that Western citizens are subject to comparable systems, albeit wrapped in the language of consumer empowerment rather than state discipline. *By pointing the finger outward, democracies avoid asking difficult questions about themselves.*

The danger of this blind spot is that it weakens the capacity for democratic self-correction. Citizens who assume that surveillance is an authoritarian problem are less likely to recognise, let alone resist, its expansion in their own societies. Governments that frame surveillance as safety, progress, or efficiency face less scrutiny, while corporations that monetise data flows are able to entrench their dominance under the guise of serving the public. The result is a slow erosion of autonomy, occurring not through sudden imposition but through gradual normalisation. The lesson is clear: freedom is not guaranteed by democratic structures alone; it depends on a cultural vigilance that democracies have too often neglected.

If authoritarian states represent the blunt edge of surveillance, democracies embody its velvet glove. Both rely on the same tools, the same behavioural insights, and the same incentives. The difference lies in perception, not substance. Until liberal societies confront their own complicity in the growth of surveillance cultures, they will continue to underestimate the depth of their entanglement. The blind spot is not merely a gap in analysis; it is a failure of imagination, a refusal to see how thoroughly surveillance has embedded itself in the democratic everyday. The challenge is not to defend freedom against a distant authoritarian other but to recognise how easily it is surrendered at home, not with a knock on the door but with a click of the mouse.

The Language of Safety and Progress

Surveillance does not advance by declaring itself as control. It advances by declaring itself as care. Systems of monitoring are rarely introduced with the vocabulary of coercion; they are wrapped instead in the rhetoric of safety, convenience, progress, and pride. This is why citizens in democratic and authoritarian societies alike so often welcome new technologies that limit their freedoms: the promise is not domination but protection, not restriction but empowerment. The framing is crucial. Few would consent to being constantly watched if the language used were about obedience or discipline. But frame the same infrastructure as a shield against terrorism, a safeguard for children, or a step toward modern efficiency, and the very same citizens who would once have resisted surveillance become its most eager advocates. *The genius of surveillance in the modern age lies not only in its technology but in its marketing.*

The 9/11 attacks provide a pivotal case study in how safety justifies surveillance expansion. In the aftermath, governments across the United States and Europe introduced sweeping new monitoring measures, from biometric passport checks to mass data collection. Programmes that once would have seemed incompatible with liberal democracies were reframed as necessary defences in an age of global terror. The Patriot Act in the United States, for example, normalised unprecedented government access to private communications. Opposition existed, but it was muted, overwhelmed by the argument that to resist these measures was to endanger the public. *Here, the language of protection shifted the burden of proof: the question was not whether surveillance should exist, but whether one was willing to be reckless enough to oppose it.*

The rhetoric of efficiency and progress plays a similar role. In workplaces, employee monitoring is rarely described as surveillance; it is framed as performance optimisation, the use of data-driven insights to help teams succeed. Digital dashboards track keystrokes, emails, and even facial expressions under the guise of improving productivity and ensuring fair distribution of labour. Few employees describe themselves as "being watched"; they are instead "being supported" or "being measured for growth." Similarly, smart cities do not promote themselves as hubs of mass monitoring but as engines of efficiency, where sensors and cameras optimise traffic flow, reduce pollution, and improve safety. Every project begins with noble language: cleaner streets, safer neighbourhoods, faster services. What fades into the background is the necessary infrastructure—vast networks of cameras, databases, and predictive algorithms—that also make citizens more visible, legible, and ultimately governable.

National pride further complicates the picture. Countries often justify new surveillance systems as signs of progress, proof of their modernity on the global stage. China's extensive facial recognition networks are presented domestically not only as tools for order but as evidence of technological leadership, a demonstration that the nation is ahead of its rivals. In Western democracies, similar narratives emerge around cybersecurity initiatives, biometric border controls, and AI-driven policing tools. These systems are framed not simply as responses to threats but as investments in the future, symbols of being on the cutting edge. Citizens who might bristle at being monitored often find comfort in believing they are participants in a shared project of national advancement. *Surveillance is thus reframed as a patriotic duty, not an imposition.*

This framing does not always deceive by accident; it often functions deliberately to blur the line between empowerment and control. A fitness tracker sold to a consumer as a tool of self-improvement becomes, in practice, a means of exporting data to insurers and employers. A home security camera marketed as protection for a family becomes part of a wider surveillance web accessible to corporations and sometimes police. At every stage, the promise of safety and convenience disarms resistance. By the time individuals notice the ways in which these devices monitor not just their environments but their habits, relationships, and movements, the infrastructure is already embedded in everyday life. *Once surveillance is embedded in routines of health, efficiency, and care, it becomes almost impossible to uproot.*

There are, of course, moments of resistance, yet even these are often co-opted by the same rhetorical frameworks. Concerns about privacy are countered with the argument that those who have nothing to hide have nothing to fear. Anxiety about data exploitation is neutralised by reminding citizens of the life-saving potential of surveillance—for instance, in tracking disease outbreaks or preventing cyberattacks. Opposition is reframed as irresponsibility, even selfishness. To challenge surveillance is, in effect, to question collective safety or to stand in the way of progress. This rhetorical inversion ensures that surveillance's critics are cast as outliers, marginalised not only politically but morally.

COVID-19 illustrates the potency of this language. In 2020, countries around the world rolled out contact-tracing apps and health-monitoring systems. Citizens were asked to share sensitive location and health data, not because governments demanded it outright, but because public health messaging framed participation as solidarity, responsibility, and care for one's community. People who may once have worried about state overreach found themselves voluntarily reporting their movements, even encouraging others to do the same. While the emergency context was genuine, the precedent was equally real: surveillance could be made not only acceptable but virtuous when linked to saving lives. What had once seemed invasive was normalised in the language of compassion and necessity.

One must recognise that the language of safety and progress is not always manipulative in intent. Governments, corporations, and communities often sincerely believe that these systems will deliver benefits. Traffic does improve with sensor data. Crime can decline with targeted monitoring. Health outcomes can be enhanced through data collection. The danger, however, lies in the cumulative effect: as citizens repeatedly accept surveillance on the grounds of efficiency, safety, or pride, they lose the capacity to distinguish between technologies that empower and those that constrain. *The very vocabulary used to justify these systems erodes the conceptual boundaries needed to defend autonomy.*

The question, then, is not simply whether surveillance protects or controls. It is whether societies can remain alert to the fact that protection and control are not opposites but often entwined. A security camera that deters crime also deters dissent. A biometric system that speeds up airport queues also feeds vast identity databases. A health app that monitors exercise can also reveal private routines to employers or insurers. When the rhetoric of safety and progress is allowed to dominate without scrutiny, it obscures these tensions, encouraging citizens to see only benefits and not trade-offs.

The central challenge for liberal societies is not technological but linguistic. Surveillance thrives in democracies because it has mastered the art of speaking the language of care. Until that language is interrogated—until citizens learn to ask what lies beneath claims of protection, efficiency, and progress—surveillance will continue to spread with minimal resistance. It is not the machinery of monitoring that blinds people to its dangers, but the words that accompany it. By the time those words are revealed as euphemisms, the infrastructures they defended will already be entrenched.

The Shared DNA of East and West

It is easy, and often comforting, to imagine that China's system of digital monitoring and behavioural control belongs to a different moral universe than Silicon Valley's sleek platforms of convenience. One projects the image of an authoritarian state intent on disciplining its citizens, while the other embodies the entrepreneurial spirit of a liberal market. Yet beneath the surface differences of rhetoric and political culture, both rest upon the same underlying behavioural logic: the use of data, incentives, and design to engineer compliance, steer choices, and limit unpredictability. The forms may differ—credit scores and state blacklists in Beijing, targeted ads and engagement metrics in California—but the function remains strikingly similar. *Surveillance capitalism and state surveillance are not opposites; they are variations on a shared grammar of control.*

Consider the Chinese social credit system. To many Western observers, it appears as a dystopian invention unique to authoritarianism: a centralised score measuring "trustworthiness," determining access to loans, travel, or opportunities. Yet the mechanics are familiar to anyone who has interacted with Uber, Airbnb, or Amazon. Ratings and reputations function as currencies of trust, where higher scores open doors and lower ones close them. The same behavioural incentives—rewarding conformity, punishing deviation—are at play. The difference lies not in the logic but in the scope: Silicon Valley platforms apply this discipline in commercial contexts, while Beijing integrates it into civic life. But the tools themselves—the dashboards, the rankings, the predictive analytics—are kin. *The cultural narratives differ, but the architecture is recognisably the same.*

The advertising model pioneered by American tech giants provides another example. Facebook and Google do not coerce users into revealing their preferences; instead, they construct systems that make voluntary disclosure irresistible. Every click, like, or search refines an invisible profile used to predict and influence behaviour. This is not far removed from China's embrace of "data-driven governance," where digital breadcrumbs—online purchases, geolocation, even friendships—are aggregated to produce forecasts of loyalty or dissent. Both systems assume that the future can be managed through predictive analytics, that society functions best when uncertainty is minimised. Whether the goal is selling a pair of shoes or preventing protest, the underlying belief is identical: *control flows from the ability to anticipate.*

Efficiency is the shared justification. In Silicon Valley, personalisation is marketed as the ultimate form of empowerment: platforms claim to save time, eliminate friction, and deliver relevance. In Beijing, efficiency is cast as collective harmony: systems promise to reduce fraud, prevent accidents, and ensure social order. Both narratives serve to obscure the disciplinary effects of the technology. When your choices are narrowed to the most profitable or most politically safe options, your autonomy shrinks regardless of whether the actor steering you is a private corporation or a public ministry. The rhetoric diverges—consumer delight versus civic responsibility—but both function to make the limitations of choice invisible. *Efficiency is never neutral; it is always structured around the goals of those who design the system.*

Nor should we underestimate the mutual influence of these systems. China has studied Silicon Valley's ability to monetise data and integrate behavioural nudges into everyday life. The design of its most successful platforms—WeChat, for instance—draws heavily on the seamless convenience perfected by American firms, while simultaneously adding features that embed state power. Conversely, Western corporations have observed how quickly citizens acclimate to constant monitoring in China and have drawn lessons about the elasticity of consent. Smart city projects in the UK or predictive policing trials in the US may not yet match the reach of Chinese experiments, but they are informed by the same conviction: if surveillance is framed as safety, convenience, or progress, resistance will be marginal. *Each side learns from the other, accelerating a global normalisation of monitoring.*

The shared DNA extends to the treatment of unpredictability. In both contexts, unpredictability is seen as inefficiency, risk, or even threat. In the West, advertisers punish unpredictability by pricing it higher: a consumer who resists profiling becomes harder to monetise and is therefore less valuable. In China, unpredictability attracts suspicion: a citizen whose movements or transactions fall outside the norm risks scrutiny or sanction. The precise consequences differ, but the underlying assumption is identical—that the healthiest society is one in which behaviour can be modelled and forecasted with minimal deviation. *Conformity is valorised, unpredictability disciplined, no matter the flag flying over the servers.*

This convergence complicates the moral binaries often drawn in public debate. Western democracies like to imagine that their surveillance cultures are fundamentally different because they are driven by markets rather than states. Yet this distinction, while real in structure, collapses when one examines outcomes: both models discipline behaviour through the same mechanisms of data collection, nudging, and ranking. Citizens in Beijing may worry about being denied a train ticket due to a low score, while citizens in San Francisco may worry about being locked out of a loan due to an opaque algorithm. Both are subject to systems that reduce human complexity to metrics, both learn to modify behaviour in response to scores, and both internalise the idea that freedom exists only within the boundaries established by unseen designers.

Indeed, the most telling evidence of this shared logic is how invisible it becomes to those who live within it. Chinese citizens speak proudly of the trust fostered by digital systems that reduce fraud or punish corruption. Western users rarely pause to consider how much of their online experience is pre-curated by algorithmic feeds. Both societies normalise their respective structures, treating them as natural extensions of modern life. And in both, the infrastructures of control advance not through overt force but through the willing participation of citizens seduced by convenience, security, or prestige. *The true convergence lies not in the technology alone but in the psychology of acceptance.*

What differentiates the two models, then, is less their essence than their scope and narrative. One claims to serve the market, the other the state. One justifies itself through the language of empowerment, the other through the language of harmony. Yet both are underpinned by a deeper continuity: the use of behavioural design to create obedient, predictable subjects. This is the shared DNA of East and West—a global behavioural architecture where political differences mask common logics of control. For those seeking to defend genuine freedom, the lesson is clear: the threat does not come only from authoritarian governments or profit-hungry corporations, but from the very idea that society should be organised around predictability, discipline, and the silent management of choice.

Case Study: COVID-19 Contact Tracing

Few episodes in modern history illustrate the speed with which surveillance can be normalised more vividly than the global embrace of digital contact tracing during the COVID-19 pandemic. Faced with an invisible and fast-moving threat, governments and corporations developed technological systems to monitor, record, and predict individual interactions on a scale previously unimaginable. What made this moment unique was not merely the breadth of adoption but the near absence of resistance: populations accustomed to framing surveillance as a menace to liberty now accepted it as a civic duty and even a form of protection. *The pandemic blurred the line between coercion and consent, making surveillance appear benevolent rather than disciplinary.*

At its core, digital contact tracing involved using smartphones to log close physical proximity between people, often via Bluetooth signals or geolocation data. If someone later tested positive for COVID-19, others flagged as having been near them were notified and urged—or in some cases required—to isolate. The technical architecture varied by country. Singapore's TraceTogether app relied on Bluetooth tokens to detect contacts; South Korea combined credit card data, CCTV footage, and mobile location logs to reconstruct the movement of infected individuals; while the UK initially experimented with a centralised data system before adopting a decentralised framework designed by Apple and Google. Despite these differences, the central feature was shared: personal data became the infrastructure for collective health. *The crisis provided a new legitimacy to the very tools that, only months before, had sparked fears of digital authoritarianism.*

In China, where strict lockdowns intersected with pervasive digital monitoring, contact tracing integrated seamlessly into an already mature surveillance ecosystem. Citizens were assigned health codes—green, yellow, or red—within mobile apps such as Alipay and WeChat. These colour-coded passes determined freedom of movement: a green code allowed access to public transport and workplaces, while red meant enforced quarantine. Though initially justified as temporary emergency measures, the logic of these passes mirrored the existing architecture of the social credit system, reinforcing behavioural conditioning. International observers were quick to characterise this as an authoritarian overreach, yet in practice, similar though less centralised systems were adopted across democracies. The supposed contrast between East and West eroded in the face of urgency. *What mattered most was not political ideology but the perceived necessity of using data to restore safety.*

In Europe, the deployment of tracing apps exposed cultural tensions. Germany, wary of its history of state surveillance, insisted on decentralised storage of contact data, ensuring that information remained on individual devices rather than being collected centrally by the state. By contrast, France initially resisted the decentralised Apple-Google framework, favouring a system that gave authorities greater oversight. These debates revealed a tension between the rhetoric of data protection and the desire for effective monitoring. Citizens were reassured that privacy safeguards were in place, yet the deeper reality was that surveillance had become the default mechanism of public health. The framing was key: rather than surveillance for discipline, it was *surveillance for care.* This reframing made acquiescence not only tolerable but morally praiseworthy.

The United States, with its fragmented federal system, relied less on centralised digital tracing and more on voluntary adoption of state-level apps, many of which failed to gain traction. Still, American citizens grew accustomed to other forms of pandemic surveillance: QR codes for vaccination verification, temperature checks linked to digital health records, and workplace apps that logged daily symptoms. Though less centralised than in Asia or Europe, the underlying shift was similar: citizens accepted forms of monitoring that, under other conditions, might have been seen as intrusive. *Emergencies collapsed the usual barriers of suspicion, making the extraordinary seem ordinary.*

The success of these systems did not depend solely on coercion. Compliance often emerged through the psychology of collective responsibility. Citizens were encouraged to download apps not for personal benefit but for the good of the community. Marketing campaigns emphasised solidarity: "protect your loved ones," "do your part," "stop the spread." The rhetoric was persuasive because it reframed surveillance as an act of altruism. This framing masked the disciplining potential of the technology. Once individuals grew accustomed to their phones silently logging interactions, the act of being monitored no longer felt alien or threatening. The psychological shift was profound: surveillance was recast from a mechanism of suspicion into an instrument of care.

Yet beneath this benevolent narrative lay deeper implications. Contact tracing systems were, in effect, real-world experiments in normalising mass data collection. They habituated citizens to the idea that their intimate social patterns—who they met, where they travelled, how long they lingered—were legitimate subjects for algorithmic processing. The data collected was ostensibly for health purposes, but it also provided governments and corporations with unprecedented behavioural maps. Critics warned that once built, such infrastructures rarely disappear. The pandemic, in this sense, accelerated the embedding of surveillance into the ordinary fabric of life. *The real legacy may not be health protection but the acceptance of constant monitoring as a default condition of modern citizenship.*

The pandemic also revealed how surveillance expands under the banner of necessity. Temporary emergency measures often harden into permanent features, justified by the possibility of future crises. Already, some governments have argued that contact tracing frameworks could be repurposed for other emergencies: natural disasters, national security threats, or new public health challenges. Once a population grows accustomed to being tracked for safety, the line between benevolent and coercive monitoring becomes indistinct. The precedent is clear: if safety is invoked, surveillance becomes acceptable. *This precedent reshapes the politics of resistance, for who dares oppose a tool framed as saving lives?*

One striking irony is that while citizens accepted unprecedented data collection in the name of health, the actual effectiveness of many tracing apps was mixed. Adoption rates often fell short of the levels needed to significantly curb transmission, and technical glitches reduced accuracy. Yet the symbolic effect of these systems was immense. They signalled that technological surveillance was the proper solution to collective risk, regardless of actual outcomes. The symbolism mattered as much as the science: societies were taught to equate monitoring with safety, even when the evidence was ambiguous. *Surveillance became less about results than about reassurance.*

The global nature of the pandemic ensured that these dynamics were not confined to a single region. From Asia to Europe to the Americas, citizens learned to scan QR codes before entering restaurants, log health data into workplace dashboards, and comply with digital gatekeepers of mobility. Differences in design and adoption existed, but the underlying lesson was universal: when fear and uncertainty are high, populations across political systems will accept surveillance not reluctantly but willingly. What was once exceptional became mundane, and what was once contested became common sense.

COVID-19 contact tracing thus provides a case study in the quiet redefinition of liberty. The pandemic revealed how swiftly and seamlessly surveillance could be reframed as benevolent, how populations could be nudged into acceptance through appeals to solidarity, and how infrastructures of monitoring, once installed, linger long after the crisis abates. The lesson is not simply about public health. It is about the political malleability of surveillance, its capacity to shift from a symbol of oppression to a symbol of care with only a change of narrative. *The pandemic did not invent this logic—it exposed how ready the world already was to embrace it.*

Chapter 6

The Economics of Compliance

Every system of control must be funded, sustained, and rationalised. Surveillance is not only a technological or political phenomenon—it is an economic one. The infrastructures that track, predict, and discipline behaviour are built upon the exchange of capital, whether in the form of corporate profit, state power, or the subtle incentives that encourage individuals to surrender autonomy in return for convenience. Compliance, in this sense, is not merely imposed; it is purchased, subsidised, and traded within a market of behavioural data. *To understand modern obedience, one must follow the money as closely as the algorithms.*

The term "surveillance capitalism" has entered public discourse to describe the model through which corporations monetise data. Every search query, swipe, and click becomes a raw material, extracted and refined into predictive products. Google's targeted advertising empire and Facebook's engagement-driven feeds are only the most visible examples. Less discussed, but equally important, are the countless apps and devices that offer "free" services in exchange for behavioural data. Fitness trackers, smart TVs, discount loyalty cards—each of these is an entry point into a system where privacy is surrendered not under duress but for perks, savings, or a sense of modern convenience. *Consumers rarely perceive themselves as being coerced; instead, they experience the transaction as a bargain in which surveillance is normalised as a price of admission to digital life.*

Governments, by contrast, use similar mechanisms of data collection but with different ends in sight. Where corporations seek profit, states seek stability, legitimacy, and control. Intelligence agencies build vast databases not to sell targeted adverts but to identify potential dissenters or threats. Tax authorities deploy algorithmic tools to detect anomalies in financial filings. Welfare systems increasingly require recipients to submit to biometric identification and digital tracking to verify eligibility. The economic logic here is not absent: efficiency and cost-cutting are frequently the justification. But the deeper logic is political: compliance is enforced not through profit motives but through the architecture of governance itself. *The same behavioural insights that allow a platform to sell shoes more effectively can also allow a government to suppress protest with surgical precision.*

The boundary between these two domains—corporate surveillance capitalism and state surveillance—has always been porous. The events of the past two decades, from the revelations of Edward Snowden to the ubiquity of corporate–state partnerships in pandemic tracking, demonstrate just how interwoven they have become. Private companies often act as both suppliers and collaborators, providing data streams to government agencies either voluntarily, under contract, or through legal compulsion. Amazon's cloud services host vast troves of government data. Palantir, a company born in Silicon Valley, powers predictive policing in the United States and Europe. Social media platforms provide real-time intelligence on protests and unrest. In these partnerships, accountability blurs: is the coercion public or private, profit-driven or political? The citizen is left with little recourse, caught between overlapping systems of extraction and control. *The merging of commercial and state surveillance produces not a simple binary but a hybrid economy of compliance, one in which profit and power reinforce one another.*

The economics of compliance is also visible in the costs borne by those who resist. Encryption, whistleblowing, and digital anonymity are often framed as acts of personal autonomy, but they come with tangible financial and social penalties. Whistleblowers frequently face unemployment, exile, or bankruptcy. Activists using secure communication platforms may find themselves excluded from mainstream tools that dominate professional and social life. Even ordinary consumers who refuse to accept data collection terms often lose access to discounts, services, or the convenience upon which modern work and socialising depend. Compliance is thus not only incentivised through perks but enforced through penalties. *Dissent carries a price tag, and few can afford to pay it indefinitely.*

This chapter examines how economics underwrites the architecture of digital obedience. It will consider how corporations and governments, despite their different aims, rely on the same behavioural data to achieve their objectives. It will show how consumers are drawn into these systems through enticements that appear benign but accumulate into a profound erosion of privacy. It will analyse the spaces where corporate and state power overlap, creating opaque systems of mutual reinforcement. And it will confront the uncomfortable reality that non-compliance is not merely a political or moral act but an economic one, with consequences that extend into livelihoods, freedoms, and futures. *Surveillance today is not only a structure of control; it is a marketplace where freedom itself is commodified.*

Surveillance Capitalism vs. State Control

The most striking feature of twenty-first-century surveillance is not simply its scale but its duality. Two parallel yet overlapping systems of data collection dominate our lives: one driven by corporations, the other by governments. Both depend on harvesting and interpreting human behaviour at unprecedented depth, yet their objectives diverge—profit in the corporate realm, power in the political. This divergence matters less than one might expect, however, because in practice the boundaries between corporate and state surveillance blur, often producing hybrid regimes where the commercial logic of monetisation and the political logic of control reinforce one another. *Understanding this dynamic is essential, for it reveals not only how individuals are tracked but also why, and with what consequences for freedom and agency.*

Surveillance capitalism, a term popularised by Shoshana Zuboff, describes an economic model in which behavioural data becomes the most valuable commodity. Corporations like Google, Facebook, and Amazon extract digital traces—search queries, clicks, GPS movements, purchase histories—transforming them into predictive products that advertisers can buy. These companies no longer sell services to users; instead, they sell users themselves, or more precisely, the capacity to forecast and shape users' future behaviour. The incentives are simple: the more detailed the data, the more profitable the prediction. A retailer that knows not only what a consumer bought last week but also what mood they are in today and what they are likely to desire tomorrow can command extraordinary precision in targeting. This is why digital corporations invest heavily in maintaining closed ecosystems—from operating systems and browsers to smart speakers and wearable devices. The aim is to ensure constant capture of behavioural exhaust, which then feeds algorithmic systems that refine control over consumer attention and desire. *Surveillance capitalism thrives not by coercion but by seduction, making its reach both expansive and insidious.*

Governments, by contrast, deploy data collection with different motives. States seek not primarily to monetise but to govern, to maintain order, detect threats, and secure legitimacy. Intelligence agencies amass telecommunications metadata to identify terrorist networks. Police forces increasingly use algorithmic systems to anticipate crime hotspots. Welfare offices demand biometric enrolment to ensure benefits are distributed only to the eligible. The justification is often efficiency or safety, framed in neutral administrative terms. But the deeper function is to render populations legible, to reduce uncertainty in governance by predicting and shaping behaviour. Michel Foucault once described the transition from sovereign power—the right to kill—to disciplinary power—the ability to regulate everyday conduct. In the digital age, data is the new discipline: those who conform to expected patterns glide through systems frictionlessly, while those who deviate find themselves flagged, delayed, or excluded. *For states, surveillance is not a market transaction but a governance imperative, though the tools are strikingly similar to those used by corporations.*

The difference in aims—profit versus power—might suggest a clear divide. Yet in practice the two domains converge. Corporate platforms, eager to preserve their market dominance, often find themselves entangled with state demands for access. The revelations of Edward Snowden demonstrated how U.S. intelligence agencies tapped into the infrastructure of major technology companies to siphon global communications. In China, the integration is more explicit: companies like Tencent and Alibaba operate under legal obligations to share data with the state, embedding commercial platforms directly into systems of political control. In Europe, even under stronger privacy regulations, private telecommunications providers routinely supply metadata to law enforcement. The resulting picture is one where the line between corporate and governmental surveillance is not a wall but a membrane, porous and frequently crossed. *When corporations and states share an interest in predictive knowledge, the citizen becomes doubly exposed—simultaneously a consumer to be exploited and a subject to be managed.*

Yet the incentives that drive these systems create distinct patterns of vulnerability. In corporate surveillance, the danger lies in the commodification of intimacy and the subtle erosion of autonomy. When every action is tracked to maximise engagement and spending, individuals are steered into behavioural ruts that serve commercial objectives rather than personal flourishing. The harm is diffuse: manipulation of attention spans, homogenisation of cultural expression, and dependency on platforms that profit from addiction. By contrast, state surveillance produces more direct and asymmetric risks. The ability of governments to freeze bank accounts, deny welfare, or pre-emptively detain perceived threats grants them a disciplinary force that corporations, for all their economic clout, cannot wield alone. *Corporate surveillance shapes desire; state surveillance polices dissent. Together, they form a feedback loop that narrows the space for unpredictability.*

This duality also explains why resistance is so difficult. Consumers may opt out of a social media platform, but they cannot easily opt out of government databases or financial infrastructures. Conversely, political opposition to state surveillance often falters because people have already normalised corporate surveillance through daily habits. If we accept that our every online purchase will be logged, that our smart speaker is always listening, it becomes harder to mount principled resistance when the state demands similar access in the name of national security. The psychological groundwork for compliance is already laid. *What begins as data-for-convenience in the market becomes data-for-obedience in the polity.*

There are moments, however, when the tensions between profit and power become visible. Apple's public refusal to create backdoors for law enforcement is one example where corporate interest in consumer trust clashed with state demands for access. Similarly, debates over encryption highlight the divergent goals: technology firms benefit from promoting security and privacy as selling points, while governments often view unbreakable encryption as a barrier to law enforcement. These tensions reveal that while corporate and state surveillance share a common infrastructure, their goals are not identical and can occasionally pull in opposite directions. Yet such resistance from corporations is the exception rather than the rule. More often, partnerships emerge: cloud computing contracts for intelligence agencies, social media monitoring for law enforcement, predictive analytics for welfare offices. *Even when profit and power diverge, they frequently find ways to converge in practice.*

The comparison between surveillance capitalism and state control is not merely academic. It illuminates the structural conditions under which obedience is engineered. In the commercial realm, we learn to comply because frictionless convenience rewards us for surrendering data. In the political realm, we comply because non-cooperation carries legal or social penalties. Each system alone is powerful; together, they form a comprehensive architecture where both desire and dissent are managed. *The future of digital governance lies in this convergence, where markets and states draw upon the same behavioural logic to secure different forms of dominance.*

To grasp the stakes, one must recognise that surveillance is not an accidental by-product of modernity but its organising principle. Corporations and governments, though motivated by different ends, are converging on the same insight: that prediction of behaviour is the ultimate currency of control. The crucial question is not whether data is collected—that is now inevitable—but to what purposes it is put, and whether societies can establish boundaries that protect agency in the face of these twin logics of profit and power.

Data as a Market Incentive

Few commodities in human history have been surrendered so readily and with so little resistance as personal data. In earlier epochs, the control of one's identity and private affairs was jealously guarded—whether through secrecy, property, or autonomy—because its loss often meant exposure to danger. Today, however, consumers routinely give up intimate information not under duress but in exchange for small conveniences, token perks, or fleeting pleasures. Loyalty cards promise discounts; fitness apps offer motivational graphs; free e-mail and social networks deliver communication without upfront cost. *The currency of modern life is not only money but disclosure, and the incentives are structured to make disclosure appear not only harmless but rational.*

The genius of data markets lies in their ability to present surveillance as reciprocity. When a supermarket issues a loyalty card, the transaction appears simple: in return for revealing what one buys, one receives coupons or small discounts. Yet the value exchange is profoundly asymmetric. The customer gains marginal savings, while the retailer acquires an extensive behavioural record—frequency of purchases, brand preferences, seasonal habits—that can be monetised repeatedly through targeted promotions, supplier negotiations, and predictive stock management. What feels like a free benefit is, in fact, the sale of behavioural predictability at a bargain price. *Consumers are not coerced into giving up their privacy; they are enticed into undervaluing it.*

The rise of digital platforms has amplified this asymmetry. Facebook, Google, and TikTok offer their services ostensibly for free, yet the business model is entirely dependent on data extraction. Users exchange their browsing histories, preferences, and social interactions for access to search, communication, and entertainment. To most, the bargain feels equitable—after all, they pay nothing. But the calculus ignores the hidden costs: the profiling of political leanings, the manipulation of emotional states, the reduction of human expression into monetisable categories. *The promise of a free service conceals the reality of commodification, where individuals themselves become the product.*

This logic extends beyond entertainment into essential services. Fintech companies lure customers with promises of no-fee banking or instant credit decisions, while in return harvesting financial data at a granularity traditional banks could never achieve. Ride-hailing apps provide affordable transport but require continuous location tracking, transforming mobility into a dataset of extraordinary value to advertisers and city planners alike. Even healthcare, traditionally guarded by strong privacy norms, has entered this exchange: insurance companies reward policyholders with discounts for wearing fitness trackers, normalising the idea that the right to affordable healthcare can be contingent on willingness to be monitored. *Incentives thus become levers of compliance, aligning personal behaviour with corporate profit goals while eroding the boundary between voluntary sharing and necessary surrender.*

It is tempting to view such arrangements as benign, a kind of marketplace pragmatism where both sides benefit. Indeed, defenders argue that consumers are rational actors, free to accept or reject incentives. If the discount is worth the loss of privacy, who is to say otherwise? Yet this framing obscures the structural power at play. The choice is rarely a genuine one: to decline data sharing often means exclusion from discounts, services, or entire platforms. The consumer may technically consent, but the asymmetry of need and bargaining power renders the consent shallow. *What is presented as choice is often closer to economic compulsion.*

The psychology of these incentives is as critical as the economics. Studies in behavioural economics demonstrate how framing and defaults shape decision-making. When data collection is linked to immediate, tangible rewards—cashback, points, convenience—the long-term, abstract cost of privacy loss recedes into the background. Few pause to calculate how a supermarket loyalty card might influence not only advertising but also creditworthiness or insurance premiums in the future. Human cognition is biased towards the present and the visible, leaving it ill-equipped to assess the opaque and cumulative consequences of data sharing. *The design of market incentives exploits these cognitive biases, ensuring that individuals consistently undervalue their privacy.*

The case of WeChat Pay in China illustrates the potency of such dynamics. By offering seamless integration of payments, messaging, and government services, the app became indispensable to daily life. Users embraced it for its convenience, scarcely recognising that every transaction, conversation, and movement became part of a state-accessible dataset. The incentive was not only discounts or perks but participation itself—membership in the social and economic fabric. Here the market incentive merged seamlessly with political control, revealing how the logics of commerce and governance can converge when convenience is the bait.

Western democracies often assume that such systems are distant, particular to authoritarian contexts. Yet the same behavioural logic underpins Amazon Prime's ecosystem. Prime customers are enticed with fast delivery, exclusive discounts, and media access. The price is not only the subscription fee but the entrenchment of consumer behaviour within Amazon's closed environment. Shopping habits, entertainment preferences, even household routines become predictable and locked into the company's architecture. What appears to be a mere loyalty programme is, in effect, a mechanism for data-driven dependency. *Convenience does not simply supplement consumer choice; it structures it, nudging individuals into paths that generate maximum extractive value.*

Contrasting views exist, of course. Some argue that data-for-services exchanges democratise access, allowing individuals of limited means to enjoy benefits without financial cost. A free e-mail service or a discounted grocery bill can matter greatly to those on tight budgets. Critics of privacy alarmism suggest that the commodification of data is no more troubling than advertising in newspapers or product placement in films. Yet such analogies underestimate the scale and intimacy of modern data collection. Newspapers never tracked eye movements; film studios never recorded heart rates; supermarkets never knew the precise time a consumer opened their fridge. *The qualitative difference lies in the depth of behavioural insight, which transforms marketing from persuasion into prediction and, increasingly, into manipulation.*

The societal implications extend beyond individual transactions. As consumers normalise trading privacy for incentives, collective resistance to surveillance weakens. A society habituated to exchange personal information for small perks is less equipped to contest intrusive state monitoring or corporate monopolisation of data. The very act of accepting discounts for disclosure reshapes expectations: privacy becomes a luxury, something to be traded rather than a right to be defended. *Market incentives do not merely exploit existing preferences; they cultivate new norms in which surveillance becomes naturalised as part of economic life.*

To understand the full scope of data as a market incentive is to see it not as an incidental feature of consumer capitalism but as its engine. Companies need not coerce individuals into compliance; they merely need to make surveillance feel rewarding. A free app, a faster delivery, a cheaper premium—these are the carrots that mask the stick of dependency, manipulation, and loss of autonomy. The subtle genius of this system is that individuals feel empowered even as they are rendered predictable, their preferences steered, and their freedom diminished. *The incentives of the market are not neutral; they are designed to reconfigure the calculus of choice itself, ensuring that privacy is always the expendable variable.*

When States and Corporations Collide

The most powerful shifts in modern governance are not enacted through parliaments or decrees but negotiated quietly in the shadows where corporate databases meet state security agencies. Surveillance capitalism and state surveillance, often treated as distinct domains, are increasingly interdependent. Corporations collect data under the pretext of convenience and profit; governments demand access to that data in the name of safety, order, or national interest. *The collision is not accidental but structural: private platforms generate the information governments crave, while governments provide the regulatory environment that sustains corporate dominance.* In this convergence, accountability fragments, leaving citizens unsure whether it is the market or the state that ultimately governs their digital lives.

Consider the case of law enforcement's reliance on Amazon's Ring doorbell system in the United States. What began as a consumer product promising homeowners peace of mind has evolved into a sprawling surveillance network accessible to police forces. Through partnerships and "Neighbourhood Watch" portals, police can request footage directly from Ring users, bypassing traditional warrants. The company frames this as empowering communities against crime, while police describe it as a cost-efficient extension of public safety infrastructure. Yet the lines blur: is the footage shared voluntarily, or is the social pressure to comply with law enforcement tantamount to coercion? *The collaboration recasts a commercial product into a quasi-public utility, yet without the democratic oversight normally required of state surveillance tools.*

Similar dynamics are visible in predictive policing. Private firms such as Palantir build the platforms, crunch the datasets, and design the algorithms, but police departments apply them in practice. The result is a diffusion of responsibility: when an algorithm misclassifies a neighbourhood as high-risk, is the fault with the company that built the tool or the police force that deployed it? Neither side is incentivised to accept full responsibility. Corporations hide behind the language of neutral technology, while states insist they are merely leveraging innovation. *The result is a governance vacuum where citizens cannot clearly attribute harm, and accountability dissipates into a fog of shared complicity.*

In China, the intertwining is more explicit. Platforms such as WeChat or Alipay are indispensable for daily transactions, yet their data flows readily into state systems for monitoring and control. To the outside world, this appears as a uniquely authoritarian arrangement, but the underlying principle is not fundamentally different from Western democracies. Facebook's data troves have been subpoenaed in criminal investigations; Google provides information to law enforcement under court orders; telecom firms hand over metadata en masse to intelligence agencies. The legal frameworks may differ, but the behavioural logic is shared: data gathered for commercial ends is repurposed for political control. *The state does not need to build its own surveillance infrastructure when the corporate sector has already done so more efficiently.*

Proponents of these partnerships argue that they are pragmatic responses to modern challenges. Terrorism, cybercrime, child exploitation—all are cited as justifications for tighter collaboration between corporations and governments. The Snowden revelations, for example, showed the extent to which the NSA relied on private telecommunications firms to access global data flows. Officials defended these practices as necessary for national security, while companies insisted their compliance was legally mandated. In both narratives, citizens were cast as beneficiaries of protection, not subjects of surveillance. Yet the sheer scale of collection revealed a deeper reality: once data exists in corporate silos, the state will inevitably seek access to it. *The incentive to merge commercial data extraction with governmental policing is irresistible when both power and profit are at stake.*

The blurring of boundaries also complicates legal and ethical oversight. Corporations operate under the logic of contracts and consumer consent, while states are bound—at least nominally—by constitutional protections and civil rights. When the two overlap, these frameworks clash. A citizen may have consented to a company storing their location data for navigation purposes, but did they also consent to that data being handed to immigration enforcement or intelligence agencies? In many cases, the law treats corporate consent as a blanket authorisation for state access. This creates a profound paradox: the rights individuals enjoy against the state can be circumvented once the state accesses their data indirectly through corporate intermediaries. *The privatisation of data collection enables the quiet erosion of democratic safeguards.*

Nowhere is this tension more visible than in the use of facial recognition. In the UK, private retailers have deployed biometric surveillance in shopping centres, ostensibly to deter shoplifting. Police then tap into these systems for their own purposes, often without explicit warrants. When challenged, police point to the retailer's right to monitor its property; retailers, in turn, suggest they are merely cooperating with law enforcement. Each actor passes the burden of accountability onto the other. Meanwhile, the ordinary citizen—whose face has been scanned, logged, and cross-referenced—has little recourse to challenge either. *What emerges is a system where surveillance is omnipresent but responsibility for it is nowhere to be found.*

To complicate matters further, the incentives of states and corporations are not always aligned. Corporations pursue profit, while governments pursue power, yet both find mutual advantage in the infrastructure of surveillance. The state gains access to data without incurring the costs of collection, while corporations gain political legitimacy and regulatory favour by positioning themselves as security partners. But these alliances can also create conflicts of interest. For example, when Apple introduced stronger encryption on its devices, it clashed directly with law enforcement demands for backdoors. In this instance, corporate profit and consumer trust outweighed cooperation with the state. Yet even here, the standoff revealed less a principled defence of privacy than a negotiation over power between two entities that both benefit, in different contexts, from data control. *The collision of interests does not eliminate collaboration; it merely reshapes the terms of it.*

Philosophically, the entanglement of corporate and state surveillance challenges traditional categories of political theory. Liberal democracies distinguish between the private and the public, the market and the state, the consumer and the citizen. But when corporations supply the data that states use to police populations, these categories collapse. Citizens become both consumers and subjects simultaneously, their digital exhaust fuelling both targeted advertising and criminal investigations. *The duality of roles—customer in the eyes of the corporation, suspect in the eyes of the state—illustrates how deeply accountability fractures in the age of shared surveillance infrastructures.*

The consequences are not abstract. Consider immigrants in the United States who have discovered that their social media posts—collected by private platforms—are monitored by immigration authorities when assessing visa applications or deportation cases. Or workers in the gig economy whose productivity metrics, generated by private platforms, are now of interest to labour regulators and tax authorities. In these cases, personal data migrates seamlessly from commercial use to political sanction, binding individuals ever more tightly to systems they never knowingly consented to join. *The portability of surveillance data across domains ensures that no boundary of life remains untouched by the entanglement of market and state.*

Ultimately, the collision between states and corporations is not a temporary aberration but a defining feature of contemporary governance. The infrastructure of surveillance is too valuable to remain confined to one domain. Profit and power, though distinct in aim, converge in practice through the circulation of data. The danger lies not simply in the existence of these partnerships but in their opacity. Citizens rarely know the extent of cooperation, let alone the specific terms of data sharing. Without transparency, accountability dissolves, and the most consequential political transformations of our time occur without debate or consent. *When states and corporations collide, the impact is not explosive but absorptive, creating a hybrid order where surveillance thrives precisely because no single actor can be held responsible for it.*

The Cost of Dissent

Resistance to systems of surveillance and control has always carried a price, but in the digital age that cost has multiplied, diversified, and in many ways become more insidious. Where dissent once demanded extraordinary acts of courage—printing banned pamphlets, standing in protest squares, refusing to obey unjust laws—today it can be as simple as encrypting one's communications, challenging a corporate platform, or leaking evidence of government wrongdoing. Yet even these seemingly modest gestures trigger disproportionate consequences. *To resist in the age of data is to step outside the currency of compliance, and the penalties for doing so often extend far beyond the individual act of defiance itself.*

Encryption offers one of the clearest illustrations. For ordinary users, adopting end-to-end encryption on messaging apps such as Signal or WhatsApp might seem like a rational measure to protect privacy. But governments increasingly frame such choices as acts of suspicion. In some jurisdictions, the very use of encryption can mark an individual out for heightened scrutiny. The paradox is striking: tools designed to secure basic digital rights can simultaneously invite law enforcement interest. In authoritarian contexts, encrypted communication can trigger surveillance warrants or even legal penalties. In liberal democracies, politicians frequently argue that encryption "goes too far," shielding criminals or terrorists. *The underlying message is unmistakable: exercising the right to privacy is itself treated as an act of dissent, with social and political costs attached to it.*

Whistleblowers face even starker consequences. Edward Snowden, Chelsea Manning, and Reality Winner represent different faces of a single phenomenon: individuals who exposed truths about surveillance or government misconduct at enormous personal expense. They forfeited careers, reputations, and in some cases, their freedom. States justify their treatment as necessary to protect national security, but the punitive response serves a broader purpose—it broadcasts a deterrent message to potential imitators. The lesson is clear: information may belong to the public, but those who release it will be punished more severely than those who conceal it. *The economics of dissent here are inverted: revealing the truth is costly, concealing it profitable.*

The financial penalties are not always formal but can be just as damaging. Protesters who take to the streets often face legal fees, fines, or loss of employment. Digital activists may find their online accounts suspended, crowdfunding campaigns frozen, or payment services withdrawn. For instance, WikiLeaks was cut off from major financial platforms such as PayPal, Visa, and Mastercard, effectively throttling its ability to operate even before legal cases were settled. These tactics exemplify how dissent can be punished not just through the blunt force of law but through the levers of financial infrastructure. *When access to digital payment systems is as essential as access to electricity, cutting someone off is tantamount to economic suffocation.*

The social penalties are equally profound. Dissenters often encounter ostracism, reputational attacks, and character assassination. Governments and corporations alike deploy narrative control to frame resisters as irresponsible, dangerous, or disloyal. Protesters may be depicted as "radicals," whistleblowers as "traitors," and privacy advocates as "paranoid." These labels are not neutral—they strip dissenters of legitimacy, eroding public sympathy and isolating them from support networks. The result is a chilling effect that extends far beyond the individuals punished: *the spectacle of punishment becomes a lesson to the wider population about the dangers of stepping out of line.*

Technology has made such penalties more efficient and enduring. Digital traces ensure that dissent is rarely confined to a moment. Employers, universities, and financial institutions increasingly consult social media histories or digital footprints before making decisions. A protest arrest or leaked tweet can follow an individual for decades, resurfacing in job interviews or housing applications. Unlike older forms of punishment, which often had clear temporal boundaries, the digital archive transforms dissent into a permanent liability. *Defiance is no longer just an act; it becomes a scar woven into one's life narrative, endlessly retrievable by algorithms.*

The penalties for resisting surveillance also reveal stark inequalities. Marginalised communities bear the brunt of the costs. Protesters in minority or immigrant communities are more likely to be targeted by predictive policing systems or have their activities criminalised. Activists in the Global South often face harsher legal reprisals and fewer protections. For them, dissent is not simply costly but existential. Yet paradoxically, these same communities have the most to gain from challenging systems that disproportionately monitor and control them. *The economics of dissent are thus unevenly distributed: those least able to afford the costs are often those most compelled to resist.*

The corporate dimension complicates matters further. Companies that present themselves as neutral platforms often wield extraordinary power in shaping what dissent is possible. App stores can ban privacy tools under the guise of policy violations. Social media platforms can algorithmically downrank activist content, ensuring it reaches fewer people. Ride-sharing apps and delivery platforms can "deactivate" workers who attempt to organise. These measures rarely appear as outright censorship; they are framed as enforcement of terms of service or community guidelines. Yet the effect is the same: dissent is punished through subtle economic and reputational channels that leave little room for appeal. *Here, compliance is engineered not through law but through the contractual fine print of digital life.*

There is also the cost borne by those who resist quietly, through practices such as digital minimalism or data refusal. Individuals who decline to participate in mainstream platforms often find themselves socially excluded. Invitations, job opportunities, and even basic services increasingly flow through ecosystems like WhatsApp, Facebook, or Google. Opting out can mean not receiving vital information or being seen as eccentric or difficult. The penalty here is not imposed directly by the state or the corporation but by peers, family, and colleagues. *The normalisation of surveillance means that those who resist it risk not only state suspicion but also social isolation.*

Philosophically, the punishment of dissent in the digital age reflects a deeper structural logic. Surveillance systems thrive on predictability, conformity, and participation. Those who encrypt, leak, protest, or refuse disrupt this logic, introducing unpredictability into systems optimised for control. Punishing such behaviour is less about the individual act and more about reinforcing the system's dominance. *By making dissent costly, the system reaffirms its power not only through the coercion of the few but through the compliance of the many who observe their fate.*

Yet the persistence of dissent, despite these penalties, reveals something equally important: resistance is never fully extinguished. People continue to encrypt, leak, and protest, even in the face of harsh consequences. The cost of dissent may rise, but so too does its symbolic value. In societies where obedience is increasingly engineered, those willing to absorb the penalties become essential reminders that freedom cannot survive without risk. *The true cost of dissent, then, is not only borne by the individual punished—it is borne by the society that allows such punishment to define the boundaries of its freedom.*

Chapter 7

The Fragility of Resistance

Resistance has always been framed as a noble constant in human history. From uprisings against monarchies to the long struggles of labour movements, there has been an enduring belief that power can be confronted in the open square, through crowds, slogans, and visible defiance. Yet when power migrates into invisible code and algorithmic systems, resistance loses its familiar target. Outrage struggles to mobilise against an adversary that cannot be seen, does not speak, and is diffused across countless platforms, contracts, and databases. Marches against governments can pressure ministers to resign; protests against platforms dissolve into hashtags that are quietly throttled by the very algorithms being challenged. *The traditional grammar of dissent has been rendered obsolete by systems that do not rely on consent in any straightforward way, but on design, defaults, and data flows.*

The failure of outrage in this new environment is not merely a question of poor tactics but of structural mismatch. Algorithmic control does not rely on dramatic acts of repression that galvanise moral opposition. It operates in the ordinary: the subtle shaping of newsfeeds, the invisible weighting of predictive scores, the quiet exclusion of some voices and amplification of others. There is no police baton to photograph, no prison cell to rally against, only the gradual constriction of possibilities and the normalisation of dependence. This invisibility denies resistance the spectacle that has historically fuelled solidarity. Outrage, once a spark for collective action, becomes noise absorbed into the system's endless churn of attention. *Protests falter not because people no longer care, but because the enemy no longer presents a face against which outrage can be sustained.*

If mass mobilisation falters, what of the myth of the lone rebel—the hacker, cryptographer, or privacy enthusiast imagined as a counterweight to sprawling systems of control? Here too, fragility is evident. Acts of individual defiance, while often ingenious, are rapidly assimilated into the very structures they sought to undermine. Encryption, once a radical defence against intrusion, is now packaged into mainstream messaging apps owned by the same corporations profiting from metadata extraction. The hacker who exposes vulnerabilities inadvertently contributes to system improvement, as companies patch weaknesses and strengthen resilience. Even acts of circumvention are monetised: virtual private networks and privacy tools are marketed as subscription products, feeding the same capitalist logics of surveillance capitalism. *The rebel's ingenuity becomes another line item in the system's budget, proof not of its fragility but of its adaptive strength.*

Collective resistance is no stronger. Privacy advocates, civil libertarians, and grassroots activists often find themselves aligned in principle but divided in practice. Coalitions fracture along ideological, tactical, or cultural lines. Some frame the problem as one of market excess, others as state overreach, still others as a question of human rights. Without a unifying vision, movements struggle to sustain momentum, fragmenting into campaigns that flare and fade. Governments and corporations exploit this fragmentation, offering minor reforms or selective partnerships to co-opt one faction while isolating others. Unlike historical struggles that rallied around tangible demands—votes for women, an end to segregation—today's battles against surveillance lack a single rallying point. Instead, resistance disperses into myriad micro-movements, each vulnerable to fatigue, compromise, or marginalisation. *Fragmentation ensures that even when many recognise the problem, few are able to align long enough to confront it effectively.*

The case of Edward Snowden remains a pivotal illustration of both the power and fragility of digital resistance. His disclosures in 2013 revealed a scale of government surveillance previously unimaginable to the general public, sparking global debate and briefly igniting reform efforts. Encryption adoption surged, legal challenges were mounted, and some surveillance programmes were curtailed. Yet a decade later, the basic architecture of data-driven control remains intact, if not more entrenched. Public outrage was real but fleeting, absorbed into the news cycle and gradually eclipsed by fresh crises. Citizens adapted to the revelations not by dismantling the system but by recalibrating their expectations of privacy. For many, the lesson was not that surveillance was unacceptable but that it was inevitable. Snowden himself became a symbol, but symbols cannot substitute for sustained structural change. *The paradox of his revelations is stark: they changed everything in terms of knowledge, yet very little in terms of practice.*

The fragility of resistance, then, is not simply a matter of insufficient will or weak tactics. It reflects the structural sophistication of systems that can absorb outrage, commodify rebellion, and outlast movements. Power no longer resides in singular institutions that can be toppled but in vast networks where accountability is dispersed. Resistance falters because it seeks to apply tools designed for one era of struggle to the architecture of another. The result is not the absence of courage or creativity but their gradual neutralisation. *The most sobering truth of our time is that even when resistance is visible, it often strengthens the very systems it opposes, feeding their adaptability and resilience.*

To understand this fragility is not to counsel despair but to sharpen analysis. If resistance is to endure, it must confront the fact that outrage, rebellion, and coalition—all once potent—now operate in a terrain designed to blunt their force. The challenge is not only how to resist but how to reimagine resistance in forms that cannot be so easily absorbed or commodified.

Why Outrage Fails

Outrage has long been the emotional catalyst of resistance. It has filled streets, overthrown regimes, and bent laws to the will of the public. The civil rights marches of the United States, the dismantling of apartheid in South Africa, or the anti-war demonstrations across Europe all relied on anger's capacity to galvanise and sustain collective action. But the landscape of power has shifted. When governance and corporate control move into invisible, algorithmic infrastructures, outrage becomes blunted, dispersed, or redirected. The machinery of influence no longer presents itself as a single targetable entity but as a distributed architecture of code, platforms, and data pipelines. Protests, no matter how loud, struggle to confront systems that are designed precisely to absorb noise without disruption. *What fails is not the human capacity for anger, but its effectiveness in a context where power operates without spectacle or centre.*

The difficulty begins with visibility. Traditional protest thrives on visibility: images of confrontation, symbols of injustice, a clear adversary. The iconic photographs of police dogs turned on marchers in Birmingham, or the tanks facing down a lone man in Tiananmen Square, condensed vast injustices into singular moments that the world could rally around. Today's algorithmic power structures leave no such images. There are no tanks on the streets when an algorithm quietly downgrades certain voices or when predictive models deny someone a loan, job, or insurance premium. The injustice lies in an absence, in an opportunity never seen, in a ranking never disclosed. Outrage seeks a face to blame, but algorithmic governance hides behind dashboards, committees, and automated systems. *The result is a profound asymmetry: power operates without being seen, while outrage depends on spectacle to survive.*

Even when outrage finds expression, it is quickly commodified. The very platforms that generate many of today's movements—Twitter, Instagram, TikTok—are built to monetise attention. A protest hashtag becomes a trending topic, which becomes advertising revenue. Viral anger, rather than destabilising the system, fuels its commercial logic. Outrage generates engagement, and engagement is profitable. Movements that once aimed to dismantle platforms end up feeding them. The Black Lives Matter protests of 2020, for instance, mobilised millions and dominated global feeds. Yet the same platforms hosting calls for racial justice were simultaneously monetising them through targeted advertising, while disinformation campaigns undermined trust in the movement. Outrage, in this sense, does not subvert the system but strengthens its core mechanism: turning collective attention into data, and data into profit.

The structure of digital outrage also lacks durability. Online activism often privileges immediacy—viral posts, hashtags, symbolic gestures—over sustained organising. Unlike union meetings, community assemblies, or long-term campaigns, digital outrage burns fast and bright, only to dissipate once the news cycle moves on. The infrastructure of surveillance and algorithmic control, however, is designed for persistence. Data accumulates, archives lengthen, predictive models refine themselves with every interaction. The contrast is stark: outrage lives in moments; control resides in systems. Movements struggle to maintain momentum against architectures that are indifferent to time and impervious to moral shaming. *The temporal mismatch ensures that even when outrage is fierce, it is rarely sustained long enough to effect structural change.*

Another reason outrage falters is that it often mistakes expression for resistance. Posting, sharing, and commenting feel like acts of defiance, but in practice they rarely alter material structures of control. The psychological release of expressing anger can even displace more difficult forms of organising. This dynamic was captured by the sociologist Zeynep Tufekci, who observed how digital platforms enable rapid mobilisation without the hard, slow work of building durable institutions. Protests erupt quickly, but because they lack the organisational backbone of older movements, they collapse just as quickly. Outrage is plentiful; infrastructure is scarce. *Expression without organisation delivers catharsis without consequence.*

Moreover, algorithmic power does not respond to outrage in the ways traditional power once did. Authoritarian states or corporate executives could be pressured by visible dissent, fearing reputational damage or loss of legitimacy. Algorithms, by contrast, cannot be shamed. They are indifferent to public opinion and immune to moral argument. Protests against predictive policing systems, for example, rarely result in dismantling the technology; at most, they lead to rebranding, minor adjustments, or promises of oversight. The system adapts, continuing to operate in the background, often with expanded capabilities. Outrage assumes that exposure leads to change, but exposure now merely feeds refinement. *In this feedback loop, every protest becomes part of the system's own learning process.*

Case studies from recent years highlight the futility of outrage when confronting algorithmic power. The Cambridge Analytica scandal revealed massive data harvesting used to manipulate electoral outcomes. Public outrage was immediate and global, with calls for boycotts and hearings. Yet Facebook's user base continued to grow, and the underlying model of surveillance capitalism remained intact. Similarly, protests against facial recognition technologies in London and San Francisco generated debate and led to local restrictions. Yet the technologies continue to expand in airports, shopping centres, and private security networks worldwide. Outrage sparks debate, but debate is not disruption; the system adapts, relocates, or repackages its practices under new names and justifications.

One of the most insidious reasons outrage fails is that it is fragmented by design. Digital platforms optimise for personalisation, meaning that two people protesting the same issue may inhabit entirely different informational ecosystems. Outrage becomes siloed into echo chambers, preventing the formation of broad-based solidarity. While one group campaigns against corporate data harvesting, another fights predictive policing, and yet another resists biometric tracking, their struggles rarely converge into a coherent movement. This fragmentation serves power well, ensuring that outrage is plentiful but divided, noisy but incoherent. *An angry public scattered into algorithmically sorted niches cannot mount the unified resistance that systemic change requires.*

There is also the problem of risk. Outrage carries personal costs, and in a world of pervasive surveillance, those costs are increasingly high. Protesters are tracked through their devices, identified by facial recognition, and monitored through social media. Employers, insurers, and governments can access or infer political behaviour from digital traces. The penalty for outrage is no longer limited to arrest or confrontation on the street; it can extend into employment opportunities, financial services, or social standing. This awareness dampens participation. Many choose silence, not out of apathy but out of rational calculation of personal risk. Outrage fails not because people are indifferent, but because they are strategically cautious in an environment where dissent is surveilled in granular detail.

Philosophically, outrage falters because it is rooted in a model of power that no longer holds. Outrage assumes power is hierarchical, visible, and embodied in individuals who can be pressured. Algorithmic control is none of these things. It is distributed, automated, and normalised into everyday life. Outrage is miscalibrated: it shouts at governments while corporations quietly shape behaviour; it targets symbols while infrastructures remain untouched. Resistance falters not because anger is weak but because it is misaligned with the mechanisms of contemporary power. *Outrage has not lost its fire; it has lost its object.*

The lesson is sobering. Outrage, once the lifeblood of collective change, has become easy to spark but difficult to sustain, powerful in expression but weak in effect. It fails against algorithmic control because such systems are invisible, adaptive, commodifying, fragmented, and resilient. Anger still matters, but it no longer carries the transformative weight it once did. For resistance to be meaningful in the age of algorithms, it must evolve beyond outrage—towards forms of organisation, solidarity, and imagination capable of matching systems that cannot be shamed, only restructured. Until then, outrage will continue to flare and fade, leaving the architecture of control untouched.

The Myth of the Tech-Savvy Rebel

The popular imagination has long lionised the lone hacker, the clever insurgent armed with code and ingenuity, capable of outwitting vast systems of surveillance and control. From cinematic portrayals of cyber renegades dismantling mainframes to journalistic profiles of "digital dissidents," the narrative of the tech-savvy rebel carries a romantic weight. It reassures us that, in the age of pervasive monitoring, there remains a crack in the system where resistance can thrive. Yet this belief is more myth than reality. In practice, individual hacks, evasions, and subversions rarely destabilise power. Instead, they are observed, studied, and often absorbed back into the very systems they were designed to undermine. *Rebellion does not stand outside the digital order; it is captured and reconfigured as part of it.*

The reason lies in the adaptive logic of digital infrastructures. Unlike traditional bureaucracies, which could be circumvented or exposed through leaks, algorithmic systems are built to learn. Each attempt to evade—whether by masking one's identity, bypassing firewalls, or encrypting communication—creates new data points for the system to analyse. Virtual private networks (VPNs), for example, once considered the preserve of dissidents and privacy advocates, are now tracked by states and corporations alike. Far from disappearing from the digital map, VPN users are flagged as anomalies, their activity scrutinised more closely precisely because it departs from the norm. What was intended as concealment becomes a marker of suspicion. *The act of resistance generates its own counter-signal, which the system internalises as part of its operating logic.*

The cycle of absorption is evident in the fate of many digital tools initially associated with subversion. Encryption, once the domain of cryptographers and activists, has become mainstream. Messaging platforms such as WhatsApp and Signal popularised end-to-end encryption, presenting themselves as shields against surveillance. Yet this very mainstreaming transformed encryption from a rebellious act into a normalised feature of communication. States adapted: some moved to regulate or ban encrypted services, others developed metadata analysis to circumvent content protection, while intelligence agencies invested in exploiting vulnerabilities at the device level. What was once a radical act of autonomy became a standard commodity, integrated into the flows of surveillance capitalism and the apparatus of state security. The rebel's innovation was not crushed but domesticated.

Consider also the spectacle of whistleblowing. Edward Snowden's revelations exposed the scale of the U.S. National Security Agency's data collection programmes, sparking global outrage. For a moment, it seemed that a single insider could destabilise the surveillance state. Yet the outcome demonstrates the system's remarkable resilience. While laws were adjusted and oversight committees convened, the core practices of mass data collection endured. Intelligence agencies expanded their justifications under the banners of counterterrorism and cybersecurity. The Snowden leaks, rather than dismantling surveillance, served to acclimatise the public to its inevitability. What had once been secret became ordinary. The rebel's act, explosive though it was, did not dismantle the system but recalibrated it. *Exposure is not escape; it is incorporation into the public narrative that ultimately legitimises what persists.*

The corporate world provides similar examples. The ad-blocking movement, hailed as a form of digital self-defence, promised to weaken the grip of surveillance capitalism by depriving companies of data and revenue. For a time, millions adopted browser extensions to block trackers and adverts. Yet corporations swiftly responded. Google, whose profits depend on advertising, integrated ad-blocking features into its Chrome browser—on the surface an act of compliance with user demand, but in reality a mechanism to privilege its own advertising ecosystem over competitors. The rebellion against advertising was absorbed, rebranded, and rechannelled into market consolidation. *What began as defiance ended as reinforcement of corporate dominance.*

The myth of the tech-savvy rebel also obscures the systemic asymmetry of resources. Individual acts of resistance operate at the scale of personal ingenuity, but they confront institutions with vast financial, legal, and technological capacity. A hacker may expose vulnerabilities in a corporation's code, but the corporation can deploy teams of engineers, lawyers, and lobbyists to neutralise the threat and even weaponise the exploit for its own advantage. The arms race is uneven: every act of evasion refines the system by forcing it to adapt, while the individual's capacity for resistance remains finite. The rebel is locked into a dialectic where their victory is fleeting, and their failure becomes the system's evolution.

Yet the allure of the tech-savvy rebel persists because it speaks to deeper cultural narratives. In Western democracies, especially, resistance is imagined through individual heroism—one figure standing against the machine. This mythology obscures the collective nature of power and, consequently, the collective requirements of effective resistance. The focus on individual evasion distracts from the systemic organisation needed to challenge structural domination. It is easier to celebrate the hacker as folk hero than to confront the more laborious task of building enduring political movements that can hold corporations and states accountable. *The myth comforts us, but it also disarms us, by locating power in individual cleverness rather than collective solidarity.*

There is also the paradox of visibility. Successful rebels often become cultural icons, but this fame itself neutralises their threat. Hacktivist groups such as Anonymous captured the public imagination in the early 2010s with their high-profile digital attacks. Yet their tactics, once startling, soon became predictable. Governments studied their methods, corporations strengthened their defences, and the group's decentralised structure made it prone to infiltration and fragmentation. What once seemed a revolutionary force was gradually reduced to spectacle—its symbolism powerful, but its structural impact limited. The rebel as celebrity becomes a figure absorbed into the culture of control, their defiance commodified as entertainment.

Perhaps most striking is how systems pre-empt rebellion by offering controlled spaces for its expression. Social media platforms, while presenting themselves as neutral forums, are carefully designed architectures that shape the contours of dissent. Activists may believe they are harnessing platforms to mobilise, but the platforms are simultaneously harvesting data, profiling users, and monetising engagement. The system does not resist rebellion; it relies on it as a source of profit and refinement. Every protest, every boycott, every subversive meme enriches the data flows that sustain the infrastructure of control. *The rebel imagines themselves as outside the system, yet their very acts of defiance become raw material for its continuation.*

This is not to deny the courage or ingenuity of those who resist. Nor is it to suggest that resistance is futile. Rather, it is to recognise the profound limitations of individual acts of evasion in a world where systems are adaptive, distributed, and deeply enmeshed in everyday life. The myth of the tech-savvy rebel risks blinding us to the need for structural strategies. Encryption, hacking, and whistleblowing may play roles in resistance, but without broader political frameworks and collective action, they are destined to be reabsorbed. The question is not whether rebels exist—they do—but whether rebellion, as currently imagined, can ever escape capture by the systems it opposes.

What emerges is a sobering paradox. Every act of digital defiance demonstrates the ingenuity of individuals and the fragility of systems, but every such act also contributes to the system's resilience by forcing it to evolve. The myth of the tech-savvy rebel endures because it offers hope. But hope without strategy is a trap. If resistance is to move beyond myth, it must shift from individual cleverness to collective redesign, from fleeting hacks to enduring infrastructures of accountability. Until then, the rebel remains not an existential threat to the system but an unwitting participant in its ongoing consolidation.

Fragmented Resistance Movements

It is a striking paradox that at a time when surveillance has become systemic, ubiquitous, and algorithmically embedded in the everyday, those who resist it remain fragmented, disjointed, and often ineffective at sustaining collective force. Privacy advocates, civil libertarians, grassroots activists, and digital rights organisations all recognise the dangers posed by data-driven governance and corporate surveillance, yet their movements rarely coalesce into enduring coalitions capable of transforming policy or shaping mainstream cultural attitudes. *The surveillance state thrives not merely on technological advantage but on the disunity of those who oppose it.*

The first obstacle is the diversity of motivations that underpin resistance. Privacy activists often approach surveillance through the lens of technical autonomy, arguing for encryption, decentralised networks, and open-source alternatives. Civil libertarians emphasise constitutional rights, legal safeguards, and institutional accountability. Grassroots activists, by contrast, frequently frame the problem in terms of economic justice, racial inequality, or labour rights, highlighting how surveillance disproportionately targets marginalised communities. While all of these critiques are valid, they often talk past each other. The cryptographer working to develop privacy-preserving protocols may not share the same language—or even the same priorities—as the activist fighting predictive policing in minority neighbourhoods. Without a common frame, these movements fail to amplify one another's causes.

A related challenge lies in the uneven distribution of technical expertise. Digital rights campaigns often hinge on complex concepts—metadata retention, algorithmic bias, biometric identification—that require specialised knowledge to explain convincingly. Activists with technical backgrounds can articulate these issues with precision but sometimes alienate wider audiences with jargon. Conversely, grassroots organisers may succeed in mobilising communities but struggle to translate their lived experience into policy-relevant arguments that resonate in courtrooms or parliaments. *The divide between the technically literate and the socially mobilised creates silos of resistance, each effective in isolation but weak in concert.*

Fragmentation is also sustained by ideological tensions. Within liberal democracies, civil libertarians frequently couch their objections in terms of state overreach, echoing a suspicion of government power rooted in Enlightenment traditions of individual rights. By contrast, some grassroots groups view corporate exploitation as the central problem, emphasising the commercial commodification of data rather than state intrusion. Still others highlight global inequalities, noting that surveillance technologies exported from the West or China are often tested first on vulnerable populations in the Global South. These competing focal points make it difficult to sustain shared campaigns. *Where one group sees surveillance as primarily a problem of liberty, another sees it as a problem of capitalism, and another as a problem of colonial power relations.* The fragmentation of focus diffuses collective impact.

History reveals that surveillance resistance is most effective when it fuses multiple domains. The civil rights movement in the United States, for example, mobilised legal strategies, grassroots protest, and cultural advocacy to shift public opinion and legislation. By contrast, contemporary digital resistance often remains compartmentalised. When Edward Snowden revealed the scale of NSA surveillance, lawyers, technologists, and activists all seized on the disclosures, but their momentum splintered into separate arenas: litigation, technical tool-building, and public education campaigns. Each achieved modest successes, yet without long-term coalition-building, the system largely endured. The lesson is stark: fragmented responses may produce sparks of resistance, but without sustained integration, they rarely alter the underlying architecture of control.

Another factor in fragmentation is the asymmetry of resources. Surveillance is institutionalised within states and corporations with budgets, infrastructure, and legal authority. Resistance movements, by contrast, often rely on precarious funding, volunteer labour, and fleeting media attention. Competition for scarce grants and public visibility breeds rivalry between groups that might otherwise cooperate. Non-profits campaign for donations, activists compete for headlines, and academics pursue publications—each carving out its own niche rather than subsuming into a broader movement. *The economics of resistance mirror the economics of surveillance: disaggregation, competition, and marketisation weaken the collective capacity for change.*

Cultural narratives also play a role in undermining coalition. In the West, resistance to surveillance is often framed as an individual responsibility—download a secure messaging app, install an ad blocker, opt out of data collection. This individualistic ethos dovetails with neoliberal notions of consumer choice, implicitly shifting the burden from systemic reform to personal vigilance. Grassroots organisers often reject this framing, arguing that privacy cannot be reduced to consumer preference when the poorest and most vulnerable cannot opt out. The clash between individualist and collectivist strategies fractures resistance further, eroding trust between groups that might otherwise find common ground.

Moreover, surveillance technologies adapt more quickly than movements can coordinate. The pandemic demonstrated this vividly: contact-tracing apps and biometric checkpoints were rolled out across multiple nations in a matter of months, justified under emergency conditions. Resistance movements scrambled to respond, but their reactions were fragmented—some emphasised health privacy, others focused on digital authoritarianism, while others framed the issue in terms of corporate profiteering. By the time coalitions had formed coherent critiques, many of the technologies were already entrenched. *The system moves at algorithmic speed, while resistance stumbles at the pace of human organisation.*

The inability to sustain coalitions is not simply a matter of internal weakness but also the result of deliberate external pressures. States and corporations often exploit divisions by framing privacy as a niche concern of privileged elites, thereby alienating working-class communities whose struggles are more immediately economic. Alternatively, they portray activists as national security risks or as disruptive radicals, thereby creating reputational costs for mainstream civil libertarians who fear association. In this way, the very act of resisting surveillance can become a source of stigma, further fragmenting movements along lines of respectability, risk tolerance, and political strategy.

Yet fragmentation is not inevitable. There are instances where alliances have formed across divides, offering glimpses of what sustained coalitions might achieve. The campaign against facial recognition technology in public spaces, for example, has united technologists, racial justice activists, and civil liberties organisations in cities such as San Francisco and Boston, resulting in municipal bans. Similarly, European debates over GDPR demonstrated how consumer rights advocates, privacy experts, and policymakers could converge on shared regulatory frameworks, even if imperfect. These cases suggest that when movements articulate a common enemy and translate their goals into accessible language, fragmentation can be overcome.

Still, the broader pattern remains one of disunity. Resistance movements rarely develop the institutional depth required to persist over decades, unlike the surveillance infrastructures they oppose. Campaigns flare in response to crises but fade as public attention shifts, leaving infrastructures intact. Without mechanisms for institutional memory and intergenerational leadership, resistance repeats its cycles of fragmentation. *The great irony of digital resistance is that in a world of networks, those who oppose surveillance struggle most to network among themselves.*

The lesson for those committed to challenging surveillance is clear: fragmentation is not merely a weakness but a structural vulnerability that power exploits. Overcoming it requires more than aligning slogans; it demands new organisational forms that bridge technical expertise, legal advocacy, and community mobilisation. Until then, the fragmented state of resistance ensures that surveillance remains not only pervasive but largely uncontested at the systemic level. The challenge is formidable, but so too is the cost of inaction: a future in which resistance is forever reduced to scattered sparks while the machinery of control burns brightly, uninterrupted.

Case Study: Snowden and Beyond

When Edward Snowden leaked a vast archive of classified documents in 2013, the revelations seemed poised to alter the trajectory of modern surveillance. Here was confirmation, in unassailable detail, that the United States' National Security Agency, in cooperation with allies and corporations, had constructed an apparatus of unprecedented scale, siphoning data not only from foreign adversaries but from its own citizens. The disclosures were explosive: entire societies were being monitored through bulk data collection, communications were being intercepted at levels that exceeded even Cold War espionage, and the distinction between friend and foe, foreigner and citizen, had collapsed under the weight of digital capability. For weeks, the global media was consumed by headlines of secret programmes—PRISM, XKeyscore, Tempora—that read like science fiction. Yet the lasting legacy of Snowden's disclosures is sobering: despite outrage, debate, and fleeting reforms, mass surveillance largely endured, and public behaviour remained remarkably unchanged. *The paradox of Snowden is that he revealed a system so sprawling and invasive that it could no longer shock us into transformation.*

The muted impact of Snowden's disclosures lies partly in the invisibility of the systems he exposed. Unlike tanks in the streets or visible police checkpoints, algorithmic surveillance leaves no daily reminders of its reach. Citizens could continue to use the same platforms, browse the same sites, and send the same emails without obvious disruption. Even when people acknowledged they were being monitored, the absence of visible consequence made it easy to relegate the revelations to background noise. Behavioural economists have long noted the phenomenon of "present bias"—the human tendency to privilege immediate convenience over abstract, long-term risks. In the case of surveillance, the convenience of free email, real-time maps, and social networks outweighed the distant risk of data interception. *The surveillance state survived not because the leaks were dismissed, but because they were absorbed into everyday inertia.*

This inertia was reinforced by political framing. Governments reacted with a mixture of defensive nationalism and cautious reform. In the United States, President Obama admitted to "potential overreach" but emphasised that surveillance was essential to national security, reassuring the public that the programmes targeted terrorists rather than ordinary citizens. In Britain, officials defended GCHQ's cooperation with the NSA as a pillar of safety against foreign threats. The debate was reframed from one of civil liberties to one of security trade-offs, where privacy became a negotiable commodity. While minor reforms were enacted—such as the USA Freedom Act, which placed restrictions on bulk collection of phone metadata—the core infrastructure of surveillance was left intact. For many, this suggested that outrage could produce incremental adjustments but not systemic change.

Snowden's leaks also revealed the complicity of corporations in the surveillance ecosystem. Programmes like PRISM highlighted how major technology companies provided direct or indirect access to user data, either under compulsion or through tacit cooperation. The shock of this revelation was tempered, however, by the lack of viable alternatives. Users outraged by corporate complicity still found themselves reliant on Gmail, Facebook, iCloud, and other services deeply integrated into modern life. Even those who turned to encrypted alternatives often discovered that their social networks, workplaces, and governments still operated within mainstream systems. The power of network effects made withdrawal from surveillance capitalism impractical for most. *Snowden's revelations exposed the trap of modern connectivity: one cannot easily exit a system that structures the fabric of daily existence.*

Media coverage played its own role in normalising the revelations. While initial reporting by The Guardian, The Washington Post, and Der Spiegel was exhaustive, public attention soon waned. Each new disclosure lost some of its shock value, blending into a pattern of revelations that seemed overwhelming in scope but impenetrable in detail. Acronyms like XKeyscore and Tempora were difficult for the average citizen to understand, reducing their emotional salience. In time, surveillance revelations became background noise—familiar, troubling, but not actionable. Media theorists have described this as the "banality of surveillance": once the extraordinary becomes ordinary, outrage dissipates. The story shifted from one of collective risk to the personal saga of Snowden himself—his escape from

Hong Kong, his asylum in Russia, his polarising image as either traitor or hero. As attention fixed on the man rather than the machinery, systemic critique receded.

Yet it would be inaccurate to suggest that Snowden's disclosures achieved nothing. They reshaped global discourse on privacy, catalysing debates about encryption, data localisation, and legal oversight. They emboldened privacy advocates and inspired reforms such as the European Union's General Data Protection Regulation (GDPR). They spurred companies like Apple to position themselves as defenders of privacy, encrypting iPhones by default and resisting government backdoors. At the same time, the contradictions were evident: even as Apple marketed privacy, it continued to profit from data-driven services and entanglements with states. The reforms, though real, were bounded by the structural incentives of both governments and corporations to maintain surveillance as a baseline. *Snowden moved the conversation, but he did not alter the underlying alignment of power.*

The limited behavioural impact of the disclosures raises uncomfortable questions about the dynamics of resistance in a digital age. If citizens cannot be galvanised by incontrovertible evidence of mass monitoring, what can? One explanation lies in the psychological phenomenon of "surveillance resignation," where individuals accept intrusion as inevitable. When surveillance is framed as the price of participation in modern society, the space for meaningful dissent narrows. Another explanation is that the risks of surveillance are asymmetrical: while its harms are diffuse and long-term, its benefits—convenience, safety, connectivity—are immediate and tangible. This asymmetry ensures that outrage is short-lived, while compliance becomes habit.

The Snowden episode also illustrates the adaptive resilience of surveillance systems. Rather than retreat, governments doubled down on justifications, framing transparency as proof of accountability rather than grounds for dismantling. Intelligence agencies adjusted their rhetoric, emphasising the legality of their operations and the oversight of secret courts. In effect, exposure was metabolised into legitimacy: if the system could withstand public scrutiny, it must have nothing to hide. The machinery of surveillance emerged not weakened but stabilised, its existence now openly acknowledged rather than covertly denied. *The paradox is that revelation did not destroy secrecy; it normalised it.*

Beyond Snowden, subsequent leaks and disclosures have followed a similar trajectory. From WikiLeaks to the Panama Papers, from Cambridge Analytica to Pegasus spyware, each revelation has produced bursts of public attention followed by gradual accommodation. Protest movements and advocacy campaigns have been launched, but rarely at scales sufficient to impose structural change. The pattern suggests that modern democracies have developed a tolerance for scandal, absorbing leaks into a broader narrative of "business as usual." Outrage becomes episodic, reform cosmetic, and the system endures.

The Snowden case study underscores a sobering lesson: information alone does not produce transformation. Even explosive leaks, backed by incontrovertible evidence, cannot compel behavioural change if structural dependencies, cultural resignation, and political framing reinforce the status quo. For resistance to surveillance to succeed, it cannot rely solely on disclosure. It must address the deeper dynamics of convenience, legitimacy, and habit that make surveillance not merely tolerated but accepted. Snowden's legacy, then, is both heroic and tragic: heroic in revealing the scale of state and corporate surveillance, tragic in showing how even seismic revelations can dissipate without altering the trajectory of compliance. *The true power of surveillance lies not only in what it collects, but in how easily its exposure can be endured.*

Chapter 8

Historical Echoes

Surveillance has always worn the face of its time. The instruments change—the quill, the file drawer, the mainframe, the algorithm—but the logic that animates them remains strikingly familiar: to watch is to rule, and to render people visible is to make them governable. Today's platforms, with their ceaseless flows of data, feel novel only in their speed, reach, and automation. Yet their DNA can be traced to earlier architectures of power. To understand the digital present, one must recognise how thoroughly it recycles the ideas, ambitions, and anxieties of earlier systems of control. The past does not merely haunt modern surveillance; it supplies its grammar.

Jeremy Bentham's Panopticon, first imagined in the late eighteenth century, remains the most enduring metaphor of surveillance for good reason. Designed as a prison in which every inmate could be observed from a single central tower without knowing when they were being watched, the Panopticon required minimal force to secure obedience. The mere possibility of being observed was enough to discipline behaviour. Today's platforms operate with similar elegance: users scroll, post, shop, and chat under the implicit knowledge that data trails are recorded and may be scrutinised. Visibility itself becomes the mechanism of control. Unlike Bentham's prisoners, however, today's participants enter willingly, seduced by entertainment, connection, or convenience. What has shifted is not the architecture but the cultural packaging. *The genius of the digital Panopticon is that it feels less like a cage than a community.*

East Germany's Stasi archives provide a second historical echo, one that underscores the sheer administrative ambition of surveillance. The Stasi maintained files on millions of citizens, cataloguing conversations, habits, and suspicions. Informants infiltrated workplaces and neighbourhoods, producing a system where citizens lived under constant fear of betrayal. Yet the system was brittle: paper files were finite, human informants unreliable, and analysis slow. Contrast this with today's databases, where every digital interaction—an online purchase, a GPS ping, a WhatsApp message—is automatically logged and categorised. Where the Stasi required armies of clerks, today's systems rely on automated indexing and machine learning. The difference is not intent but capacity. What the Stasi achieved with labour and intimidation, modern databases accomplish invisibly, continuously, and at scale. *If the East German model instilled obedience through suspicion, today's systems normalise it through frictionless data capture.*

Colonial history offers yet another precedent, showing how information has long been a tool of domination. Empires were not maintained only by military might but by the quieter infrastructure of enumeration. The British census in India, for instance, categorised populations into religious and caste groups, transforming fluid identities into rigid administrative labels that could be policed. Passbooks and identity cards in colonial Africa turned mobility into a privilege contingent on paperwork. Maps, censuses, and registries allowed empires to segment, tax, and discipline populations more effectively than force alone. These proto-surveillance systems foreshadowed today's databases: to catalogue people is to control them. What is distinctive about the digital age is that enumeration no longer arrives sporadically, through census or checkpoint, but continuously, through sensors and networks. The imperial census produced a snapshot; today's platforms generate a live feed.

Yet to dwell only on continuity risks missing the rupture. The digital surveillance of today is not merely a more efficient Panopticon, a scaled-up Stasi, or a globalised census. It is a qualitatively new formation built on real-time feedback loops and global interconnection. Algorithms do not just observe behaviour; they modify it by curating feeds, recommending purchases, and predicting actions. Surveillance is not a static archive but a dynamic system of nudges and reinforcements. A search query reshapes future suggestions, a purchase alters creditworthiness, a social post influences visibility in a network. The feedback is instantaneous, personal, and inescapable. Furthermore, unlike the bounded reach of prisons, states, or empires, digital platforms operate transnationally, transcending borders even as they feed national security agendas. *What distinguishes the present from the past is not the desire to watch, but the capacity to intervene in real time, at scale, and without clear limits.*

Historical echoes remind us that surveillance has never been an aberration but a recurrent strategy of governance. Each era finds new justifications—rehabilitation, national security, imperial order, consumer convenience—but the underlying principle is constant: those who design systems of visibility shape the conditions of freedom. To treat digital surveillance as an unprecedented novelty is to underestimate its lineage. To treat it as mere continuity is to overlook its transformation. The task, then, is to see both: how today's architectures are haunted by the logics of earlier systems, and how they surpass them in speed, subtlety, and scope. In making sense of the present, the past is not a distant mirror but a living context, one that reveals the perennial tension between visibility and autonomy, between the power to watch and the right to live unobserved.

From Panopticon to Platform

Jeremy Bentham's Panopticon, conceived in the late eighteenth century, was never built to its full specification, but its shadow has long outlived its blueprints. Bentham imagined a prison arranged in a perfect circle, with a central watchtower from which guards could observe every inmate. The architecture was designed so that prisoners could never know whether they were being watched at any given moment, compelling them to internalise surveillance as though it were constant. Control here was not exercised through chains or whips but through uncertainty, visibility, and the possibility of observation. Bentham's idea has since become shorthand for a broader logic of governance, one that relies not on overt force but on *self-regulation under the gaze of authority.* The relevance of this eighteenth-century design in the twenty-first-century digital landscape is not incidental. It points to a continuity: the essential logic of surveillance as a tool for shaping behaviour persists, even as its mediums have evolved from prison walls to digital platforms.

What makes Bentham's design so enduring is not its physical structure but its psychological insight. The prisoner becomes both subject and enforcer of discipline, modifying behaviour without the need for direct coercion. This model reappears, in subtler and more pervasive forms, in the architecture of digital platforms. The likes of Facebook, TikTok, Google, and Amazon do not need to punish users for misbehaviour. Instead, they structure environments where visibility—through metrics, tracking, and algorithms—gently but firmly disciplines behaviour. A user posting on Instagram becomes both the observed and the observer, curating their self-presentation in anticipation of the algorithm's rewards or penalties. The fear of an empty "like" count or reduced reach replaces the guard's gaze. *Just as Bentham's prisoners adapted to perpetual potential visibility, today's users calibrate their actions to the invisible metrics that decide what surfaces, circulates, and disappears.*

The leap from Panopticon to platform is not a simple metaphorical flourish; it is an operational transformation. Platforms do not merely replicate Bentham's logic—they expand it. In the Panopticon, visibility was one-directional: guards watched inmates. In digital architectures, visibility becomes multi-directional and participatory. Users not only adjust to being watched but actively watch one another, producing a horizontal surveillance that reinforces conformity. Peer monitoring, amplified through comment threads, follower counts, and public metrics, creates an environment where the community itself sustains the platform's disciplinary effects. What was once the guard's task is now distributed among friends, strangers, and algorithms alike.

This expansion brings an important shift: platforms make participation voluntary, even desirable. The Panopticon was a prison; digital platforms are designed to feel like spaces of play, convenience, and connection. The brilliance of their architecture lies in obscuring the power dynamics embedded within them. Surveillance becomes consensual because it is wrapped in the language of engagement. Location services promise better restaurant recommendations, smartwatches promise healthier living, and social media promises visibility and relevance. Few recognise that, in offering data, they are also enrolling themselves in a system of behavioural discipline. *The Panopticon coerced through fear; the platform persuades through desire.* Yet the outcome is structurally similar: both produce predictable, compliant subjects.

The Panopticon also clarifies why resistance in platform environments often falters. In Bentham's model, refusing to comply meant risking exposure or punishment. In platform architectures, dissent manifests as invisibility. Algorithms downgrade content that disrupts established norms or challenges commercial interests. Activist campaigns may trend briefly but are quickly buried once they stop producing profitable engagement. The architecture itself ensures that only certain forms of behaviour are rewarded with visibility. Silence is not imposed by force but generated by design. This recalls Michel Foucault's reinterpretation of Bentham: the Panopticon was not merely a prison design but a metaphor for the diffusion of power throughout modern institutions. Digital platforms are the latest manifestation of this diffusion, embedding power into the very design of interaction.

A striking aspect of the transition from Panopticon to platform is the scale and subtlety of modern visibility. Bentham's design could house hundreds of prisoners at most. Today's platforms manage billions of subjects, and unlike the prison, the watchers are not clearly identifiable. Algorithms replace guards, processing behaviours invisibly, learning from patterns, and adjusting outcomes in real time. This absence of a human watcher destabilises traditional ideas of accountability. One cannot appeal to an algorithm in the way one might petition a guard. The rules of visibility and invisibility are opaque, proprietary, and often impervious to scrutiny. *In the digital Panopticon, power is not centralised in a tower but dispersed across code, protocols, and corporate servers.*

It is also worth noting the feedback loop that distinguishes platforms from Bentham's original design. In the prison, observation was passive; the guard noted but did not immediately alter the prisoner's behaviour. On platforms, observation is inherently active. Every click, pause, or swipe feeds into a system that recalibrates what will be shown next. The prisoner becomes not only observed but continuously nudged. Behaviour is not merely watched but actively shaped, with each action reinforcing the predictive capacities of the system. This is a level of control Bentham could not have imagined: surveillance that not only disciplines but *anticipates*, and in doing so, quietly governs the future trajectory of choice.

The continuity from Panopticon to platform thus lies in the logic of visibility as control, but the divergence lies in its sophistication. Where Bentham required architecture, modern platforms require only design patterns and invisible code. Where the Panopticon instilled fear, platforms manufacture desire. Where the prison compelled compliance by threat, digital spaces engineer compliance through incentives and habituation. Yet the underlying aim remains constant: to render subjects legible, predictable, and governable by structuring the conditions of their visibility. This persistence suggests that surveillance is less a historical aberration than a recurring solution to the perennial problem of governing populations.

Recognising this continuity does more than satisfy intellectual curiosity. It sharpens our understanding of why digital platforms are so effective at producing compliance and why critiques of surveillance often fail to shift behaviour. People do not resist what they do not recognise as coercion, and platforms are designed precisely to naturalise their control. By framing visibility as empowerment and participation as choice, they recast discipline as self-expression. The Panopticon's prisoners were acutely aware of their subjugation; platform users often mistake theirs for freedom. *This is the great paradox of surveillance today: its most powerful forms no longer feel like surveillance at all.*

From Bentham's circular prison to Silicon Valley's global platforms, the thread that connects them is a simple but profound truth: visibility is never neutral. To be seen is always to be shaped. The transformation from Panopticon to platform does not mark a break with the past but a refinement of its most enduring mechanism of control. Those who design the architectures of visibility—whether in stone or in code—determine not only what can be seen but what can be done. The question that remains is whether we, as subjects of these systems, can learn to see the structures that claim to see us.

The Stasi and the File Drawer

In the final years of the German Democratic Republic, the headquarters of the Stasi in East Berlin contained a labyrinth of corridors stacked high with filing cabinets. Inside them were the lives of citizens in fragments: love letters confiscated from the post, reports from neighbours recruited as informants, school records, workplace evaluations, intercepted telephone transcripts, and handwritten observations of daily routines. At its peak, the Ministry for State Security employed nearly 100,000 staff and commanded the loyalty of an estimated 200,000 informants. The Stasi is often remembered as a bureaucracy of paranoia, one that smothered its own citizens under the weight of paper. Yet, compared to the digital infrastructures of the twenty-first century, the Stasi's file drawers appear almost primitive. Where the East German state struggled with scale, speed, and accuracy, today's surveillance systems—run by corporations as well as governments—achieve the same ends with subtlety, efficiency, and automation. To compare the two is not to diminish the trauma of life under East German surveillance, but to underscore a historical continuity: the impulse to catalogue, to predict, and to discipline populations has merely shifted medium, not intent.

What stands out in retrospect is the sheer inefficiency of the Stasi's paper regime. Files were meticulously written, copied, and indexed by hand. Entire careers were spent managing the mechanics of collection: typewriters clattering through the night, folders stacked precariously in overcrowded basements, and couriers shuttling documents between regional offices. Information gathered through postal interception or covert listening devices could take days or weeks to be filed, retrieved, and assessed. Decisions were often delayed by the mechanics of bureaucracy itself. Yet for all its inefficiency, the archive served its purpose: it created a sense among citizens that nothing was private, that every interaction might be recorded and preserved. Fear did not depend on the immediate processing of data but on the knowledge that a file with one's name existed somewhere in those drawers.

Contrast this with today's databases, where scale and speed eclipse anything imagined by East German officials. The Stasi kept records on perhaps one-third of its population, amounting to millions of files. Facebook alone can track billions of individuals in real time, recording their clicks, preferences, social connections, and movements with precision the Stasi could only dream of. Where East German citizens might have taken comfort in the physical limits of the archive—its reliance on human labour, its vulnerability to error—modern surveillance operates with machine learning and predictive analytics, producing insights at scale with little human intervention. The citizen today is not only recorded but modelled, their future behaviours inferred from past data. The file drawer has been replaced by the database, and with it comes a transformation in both subtlety and effect.

The speed of digital surveillance introduces a qualitative change that reshapes how power operates. Stasi files were retrospective: they documented what had already occurred. A file might reveal that a worker expressed discontent in a factory meeting, or that a student voiced anti-state sentiments in a letter to a friend. Intervention came after the fact. By contrast, modern databases are prospective. They allow interventions before behaviour materialises. A flagged keyword can trigger automated alerts to security agencies; a shift in online browsing habits can prompt targeted advertising or algorithmic content curation. This temporal shift—from after the act to before—marks a profound difference. Surveillance no longer merely observes; it anticipates, nudges, and in doing so closes off futures before they have even been realised. *The file drawer documented dissent; the database predicts and neutralises it.*

Equally significant is the subtlety with which surveillance is now embedded in everyday life. In East Germany, citizens were acutely aware of being watched. The presence of informants was suspected, letters arrived resealed, and phone lines often crackled suspiciously. Surveillance was a blunt instrument, designed as much to intimidate as to gather intelligence. Today's citizens, by contrast, are often complicit in their own monitoring. They carry smartphones that track location, wear fitness devices that log heart rates, and volunteer personal details to platforms in exchange for convenience or entertainment. The data that feeds into vast corporate and state databases is given willingly, even enthusiastically. Surveillance has shifted from coercion to consent—or rather, to the illusion of consent, since the alternative to participation is often exclusion from the conveniences of modern life. *Where the Stasi operated in shadows, modern systems thrive in the open, normalised as infrastructure.*

This comparison also reveals how accountability is diffused in the digital age. Stasi files, however oppressive, were at least traceable to an identifiable apparatus of the state. They bore the handwriting of officials, the stamps of ministries, the signatures of case officers. In today's environment, responsibility is harder to locate. A predictive policing algorithm might rely on data purchased from a private broker, collected from consumer apps, and processed by machine learning models developed by third-party contractors. Who, then, is accountable for an error? The opacity of algorithmic systems makes it difficult to determine where surveillance originates, who controls it, and who benefits. Citizens are left navigating an invisible web of watchers, none of whom can be easily confronted or held responsible.

The comparison between file drawers and databases also highlights the question of permanence. Stasi files were material and finite. They could be burned, shredded, or left to decay in mouldy basements, as many were after the fall of the Berlin Wall. Their fragility offered the faint possibility of disappearance. Digital data, by contrast, resists decay. Stored across redundant servers and backed up in multiple locations, personal information now has a permanence that transcends individual lifespans. Even deletion is illusory, since copies often remain cached or archived elsewhere. This durability of data intensifies its disciplining power: citizens must now live with the knowledge that digital traces cannot be fully erased. The file drawer was heavy with paper; the database is weightless, yet far more enduring.

Some might argue that comparisons with the Stasi risk overstating the dangers of contemporary systems. After all, liberal democracies operate under different political frameworks than one-party states, with judicial oversight, press scrutiny, and civil society advocacy. But the historical echo remains instructive. The Stasi did not rely on advanced technology; it relied on an idea—the idea that the state must know its citizens intimately in order to manage them. That same logic drives the accumulation of data today, whether by governments seeking security or corporations seeking profit. What differs is not the underlying principle but the *ease and subtlety with which it can now be executed.* If East German citizens lived under the weight of visible files, today's global citizens live under the weight of invisible datasets whose reach is greater precisely because it is less apparent.

To dwell on this continuity is not to claim that nothing has changed, but rather to insist that scale, speed, and subtlety alter the nature of surveillance in ways that require vigilance. The Stasi's archives remind us that surveillance, once exposed, can become a moral and political scandal. The challenge of the digital age is that the archives are invisible, distributed, and defended not only by governments but also by the incentives of global markets. The metaphor of the file drawer is useful here: it allows us to see how a logic of accumulation persists, even as the drawer expands into the boundless capacities of the cloud. The lesson of history is not that surveillance was worse then than now, but that the mechanisms of observation always adapt to the tools available. Today, those tools are faster, subtler, and far more entangled in the fabric of daily life.

The image of grey filing cabinets stuffed with the intimate lives of East Germans remains a chilling reminder of how deeply surveillance can penetrate society. Yet the greater lesson lies in recognising that we have built systems of our own that surpass those cabinets in every dimension—except, perhaps, in visibility. The Stasi's files could be walked through, photographed, eventually opened to public scrutiny. Our databases, by contrast, are sealed behind corporate walls, encrypted not for the protection of citizens but for the protection of proprietary interests. To remember the Stasi is to remember that surveillance is never neutral, and that the archive, whether physical or digital, is always a weapon of power. What was once handwritten in drawers is now encoded in databases, but the underlying imperative remains: to render human lives transparent to those who govern them.

Colonial Precedents of Control

Modern surveillance is often framed as the product of digital innovation, a technological revolution born of algorithms, big data, and global networks. Yet long before satellites hovered above cities and biometric scanners verified identities, empires were refining instruments of visibility and control through more rudimentary, but no less consequential, techniques. The census, the map, and the identity document—tools often presented as administrative conveniences—were in fact foundational mechanisms by which colonial powers rendered subject populations legible, governable, and ultimately compliant. These proto-surveillance systems did not rely on digital code, but on the same underlying logic that animates today's platforms: that power resides in the ability to observe, classify, and intervene in the lives of individuals and communities.

The census is a prime example of this convergence between governance and surveillance. To count a population is to claim authority over it. British colonial censuses in India illustrate this dynamic with particular clarity. Beginning in the mid-nineteenth century, the British administration embarked on decennial enumerations not simply to record numbers, but to fix identities. Communities were divided into rigid categories of caste and religion, often reducing complex and fluid social realities into neat, administrative boxes. These classifications were not neutral. By inscribing caste hierarchies into official records, the colonial state deepened and institutionalised divisions, thereby strengthening its capacity to govern by exploiting fissures within Indian society. *The census was never only about counting bodies; it was about defining them in ways that made them more manageable for the state.* What looked like objective data collection was in fact a project of political ordering, shaping the very identities it purported to describe.

Mapping functioned in a similar way. The imperial cartographer's task was not merely geographical; it was deeply political. Maps produced under colonial rule often redrew boundaries, reclassified territories, and imposed new notions of ownership and jurisdiction. In Africa, for instance, European empires used mapping to carve arbitrary borders that split ethnic groups and lumped together disparate communities, creating states whose borders still fuel conflict today. Mapping enabled resource extraction—forests catalogued, rivers charted, mineral deposits marked—and facilitated military campaigns. But beyond strategy, mapping produced a visual narrative: the vastness of empire condensed onto a sheet of paper, with colonial power inscribed in lines and symbols. The act of seeing from above, of reducing territory to a manageable grid, reflected the same logic later embedded in satellite surveillance and aerial drones. The map rendered colonised space legible not to its inhabitants but to those who ruled them.

Identity documents provided a more personal, granular mechanism of control. Pass systems, travel permits, and identification papers allowed colonial states to track, restrict, and discipline movement. In apartheid-era South Africa, the infamous passbook determined where Black South Africans could live, work, or travel, effectively transforming mobility into a privilege granted at the discretion of the state. Earlier, in colonial Kenya, the British introduced the kipande system—a compulsory identity document worn around the neck—that recorded employment history and could be used to control labour mobility. Such documents tied individuals to fixed identities within bureaucratic structures, making them traceable and governable. Resistance often targeted these very instruments: burning passes became a symbolic act of defiance. Yet the enduring lesson is that identity systems, framed as practical necessities for administration, often served as shackles binding individuals to state oversight.

What these colonial precedents reveal is that surveillance has always been entangled with narratives of improvement, order, and progress. The census was justified as a tool for better governance, the map as a contribution to knowledge, the identity document as an enabler of security and efficient administration. But behind these rationalisations was the same asymmetry of power that characterises contemporary surveillance regimes. Colonised subjects had little say in how they were counted, classified, or tracked, just as today's citizens have limited ability to challenge the data categories imposed on them by platforms or governments. The ideological framing—that these tools were for the common good—masked their coercive edge. *Surveillance, even in its most bureaucratic forms, is rarely imposed as surveillance; it arrives clothed in the language of rationality and benefit.*

It is tempting to view these colonial systems as blunt instruments compared to the precision of modern databases, yet their psychological and social impact was no less profound. To be reduced to a caste category by the census, to see one's land redrawn on a foreigner's map, or to be forced to carry an identity pass was to live under the constant reminder that one's autonomy was circumscribed by the state. The act of enumeration, mapping, or documentation was not merely technical—it was symbolic. It communicated that subjects were known, tracked, and subordinated within a framework they did not control. In this sense, the colonial experience prefigures the sense of exposure and constraint many feel today under digital surveillance, though the mechanisms have become subtler and more pervasive.

The continuity between colonial and digital control lies in the interplay between visibility and vulnerability. Colonial powers sought to render populations visible in order to govern them; today's corporations and states pursue visibility through data for purposes of profit and security. The shift is one of scale and sophistication, not of underlying logic. Where the British Raj might have taken years to compile a census report, a tech company can now analyse a user's behaviour in real time. Where colonial maps imposed rigid borders, digital maps track movements dynamically, tracing not just where people are but where they are likely to go. Where passbooks restricted physical mobility, biometric IDs and algorithmic risk scores restrict access to services, loans, or jobs. The technologies differ, but the governing principle—that to be seen is to be controlled—remains constant.

At the same time, the comparison highlights a tension worth probing. Colonial surveillance was overt and often brutal, leaving little ambiguity about its coercive function. Today's systems, by contrast, thrive on subtlety and voluntariness. People eagerly fill in online forms, share location data, and authenticate themselves with biometric scans, often perceiving these acts as conveniences rather than impositions. The genius of modern surveillance is that it rarely presents itself as domination; it disguises itself as empowerment. And yet, this is precisely what makes it more effective than its colonial antecedents. Consent becomes a lubricant for control, smoothing the rough edges of power. *If colonial subjects were surveilled in spite of themselves, modern citizens are surveilled with their own participation.*

To study colonial precedents of control is therefore to recognise that surveillance is not a historical aberration of the digital age, but a recurring feature of how power organises knowledge about populations. The census, the map, and the identity document were not neutral tools but political technologies, foreshadowing the datafication of life we witness today. They remind us that surveillance has always been justified as administration, and that its most enduring danger lies not in its novelty but in its normalisation. The lesson is not that our current systems replicate colonialism in form, but that they share its DNA: the drive to see, to categorise, and to constrain. The medium has changed, but the ambition remains.

Why Today's Systems Are Different

What distinguishes today's surveillance systems from their historical predecessors is not simply their technical sophistication, but their velocity, ubiquity, and invisibility. Where past regimes of control relied on files, maps, and paper archives, the digital infrastructure of the twenty-first century operates through continuous flows of data that feed back into the very systems that generate them. This dynamic creates a form of surveillance that is not only more comprehensive than anything previously imagined but also more adaptive, responsive, and difficult to resist. *The shift from static records to real-time feedback loops marks a qualitative transformation in the architecture of control.*

One of the most striking differences is the immediacy of digital surveillance. The East German Stasi maintained sprawling archives that could take months to collect and analyse, but a search of their records was always retrospective, locked in time. By contrast, today's platforms and governments capture information at the moment it is produced. Every click, search, or swipe is logged, and that data can immediately influence what the user sees next—be it an advertisement, a news story, or a police alert. The speed of this cycle collapses the gap between observation and intervention. Surveillance is no longer about archiving behaviour for future use; it is about shaping behaviour as it unfolds. *Power now operates in real time, inserting itself into the stream of life rather than arriving after the fact.*

Global reach intensifies this transformation. Colonial empires and authoritarian states may have controlled vast populations, but their reach was ultimately bounded by geography and logistics. Digital systems, however, are borderless by design. A social media platform headquartered in California can influence elections in Africa; a payment processor in Singapore can track the spending habits of customers in Europe; a messaging app in China can shape social interactions across continents. The infrastructures of visibility now stretch across jurisdictions, often eluding regulation and accountability. This global scope does not merely expand the scale of surveillance; it fuses disparate domains of life into a single networked field, making individual resistance increasingly difficult.

Equally important is the role of algorithmic feedback. Traditional surveillance collected information passively; it was the analyst, the bureaucrat, or the secret police officer who made decisions based on the files. Today, machine learning systems draw inferences from data at a speed and scale no human could match, adjusting outputs on the fly. Recommendation engines learn from a user's behaviour and nudge them towards further engagement, while predictive policing software anticipates crime and reallocates resources accordingly. The key feature is reflexivity: systems that not only observe but also reshape the environment in which behaviour takes place. *This constant loop between input and output means surveillance is no longer an external imposition but an embedded condition of everyday interaction.*

Consider the case of predictive policing platforms deployed in cities such as Los Angeles and Chicago. Data on past arrests and reported crimes is fed into algorithms that claim to predict future hotspots of criminal activity. Police are then directed to patrol those areas more heavily, leading to more arrests, which in turn reinforces the algorithm's predictions. This feedback loop not only entrenches existing patterns of surveillance but also amplifies them, creating a self-fulfilling cycle. Unlike earlier forms of policing, which relied on static intelligence, today's systems adapt and evolve in response to their own outputs, making them harder to challenge and more opaque in their operation.

The economic incentives driving these systems further distinguish them from their historical forebears. Surveillance under authoritarian regimes was primarily about political control. In the digital age, however, commercial motives fuse with state objectives. Technology companies are not just passive collectors of data but active participants in shaping the attention economy. Social media platforms fine-tune their algorithms to maximise user engagement because attention translates directly into advertising revenue. This financial logic aligns with the state's interest in maintaining social stability and monitoring potential threats, leading to partnerships where commercial and governmental goals converge. *The surveillance economy does not merely coexist with state surveillance; it amplifies and legitimises it under the guise of efficiency and innovation.*

Another distinguishing feature is the invisibility of digital surveillance. Colonial censuses, identity documents, and police files were palpable artefacts of control; their coercive intent was rarely in doubt. By contrast, contemporary systems often present themselves as conveniences. Facial recognition at an airport is framed as a way to speed up boarding, health-tracking apps as tools of empowerment, smart devices as sources of comfort and efficiency. This veneer of benevolence masks the extent to which data is continuously extracted and repurposed. The more seamless the technology, the less visible its surveillance function becomes. *The most powerful forms of control today are not those that announce themselves, but those that disappear into the fabric of daily life.*

The social consequences of this new architecture are profound. In past surveillance states, individuals could adopt strategies of avoidance—burning passes, refusing censuses, or meeting in secret. While risky, such acts allowed for moments of defiance. In today's systems, resistance is complicated by the fact that participation is voluntary in appearance but mandatory in practice. Opting out of social media may mean exclusion from professional and social networks; rejecting smartphone apps may restrict access to services; refusing biometric identification may make one illegible to the state altogether. The price of resistance is higher precisely because surveillance is woven into the very infrastructure of modern life.

Critics might argue that the sheer volume of data makes meaningful surveillance impossible, that the noise outweighs the signal. Yet this underestimates the power of automated analysis and the incentives driving continuous data capture. The point is not that every piece of data will be scrutinised by a human observer, but that data will be stored, cross-referenced, and made available to algorithms that can detect patterns invisible to individuals. Even when not actively monitored, the possibility of monitoring creates a chilling effect. People moderate their behaviour online and offline, conscious that their actions are recorded. The Panopticon effect—visibility as discipline—no longer requires a central tower; it is embedded in the architecture of platforms that promise connection and efficiency.

What makes today's systems unprecedented, then, is not a single breakthrough but the convergence of several qualities: speed, scale, reflexivity, invisibility, and economic entanglement. Together, these create a surveillance environment that is continuous, adaptive, and global in scope. Unlike the archives of the Stasi or the census forms of empire, digital systems do not simply record; they intervene. They shape attention, guide movement, allocate resources, and define opportunities in real time. They blur the distinction between voluntary and coerced participation, between empowerment and exploitation. They make surveillance not an exceptional feature of authoritarian rule but the default condition of everyday life across democracies and autocracies alike.

Understanding why today's systems are different is not merely an academic exercise; it is essential to recognising the new terrain of power. The tools may bear a superficial resemblance to their historical predecessors, but their operation is profoundly distinct. They do not simply watch; they act. They do not simply record the past; they shape the present. And they do not confine themselves within national borders; they extend everywhere digital infrastructure reaches. *The defining feature of modern surveillance is not its existence, but its totalisation—the fact that it now pervades the very structures through which people live, work, and relate to one another.*

Chapter 9

Everyday Obedience

The most enduring forms of control are rarely enforced with violence or overt coercion. They persist because they are naturalised, folded seamlessly into the fabric of daily routines until compliance no longer feels like submission but common sense. The modern individual does not need to be forced into obedience; instead, they are nudged, tracked, and normalised into patterns of behaviour that serve organisational, corporate, and political ends. What makes this condition striking is its banality. Obedience today is not demanded in the shadows of prisons or under the threat of authoritarian police powers but through dashboards at work, devices at home, and apps that parents download with the hope of keeping their children safe. *The genius of contemporary systems of surveillance is that they make obedience appear voluntary, rational, and even desirable.*

Workplace monitoring provides one of the clearest illustrations of how this has taken root. In earlier decades, supervision involved a manager walking the floor, observing staff performance, or reviewing end-of-day reports. Today, millions of workers log into platforms that monitor their keystrokes, track idle time, or generate productivity scores. Biometric systems clock employees in and out, while AI-driven cameras detect posture or facial expressions in warehouses and call centres. The metrics then feed into performance dashboards that are not only visible to management but, in some cases, shared with employees as motivational tools. What was once oversight has become self-surveillance, with workers internalising the metrics by which they will be judged. Resistance becomes difficult not because penalties are severe but because the system is presented as efficient, fair, and data-driven. *The workplace thus functions as a training ground in which obedience is rationalised as productivity, and surveillance is reframed as transparency.*

Beyond the office or factory floor, obedience infiltrates the private sphere through the rapid diffusion of "smart" technologies. Voice assistants, thermostats, and cameras installed for convenience or security collect constant streams of data on household routines. These devices do not simply record; they shape behaviour by rewarding certain actions with ease and punishing others with friction. A home with automated lighting and heating adapts to its occupants' movements, but it also conditions those movements by setting patterns that feel natural over time. When people adjust their schedules to align with their devices rather than the reverse, they are no longer merely using technology—they are being subtly disciplined by it. The trade-off is rationalised as comfort, yet the result is a household structured by systems that both serve and monitor. *The home, long imagined as a private refuge, becomes another arena in which obedience is quietly engineered.*

Perhaps the most significant normalisation of surveillance begins in childhood. Parenting apps, location trackers, and digital monitoring tools are often marketed as means of safety, offering parents reassurance and control in a world perceived as uncertain. Yet these tools also habituate children to being tracked, evaluated, and held accountable to invisible systems. A generation is growing up in which constant visibility is not an exception but an expectation. By the time these children enter the workforce, the transition to employer monitoring or state databases will feel less like an intrusion and more like continuity. What began as a parental gesture of care matures into a lifelong architecture of obedience. *Surveillance in childhood is not only about control in the moment; it is an investment in cultivating compliance as a default orientation towards authority.*

This embedding of surveillance into daily routines makes it profoundly difficult to resist. Unlike earlier forms of control, which were visible and could be confronted through protest or avoidance, today's mechanisms of obedience are ordinary, even banal. A person who questions productivity software may be cast as resistant to modern efficiency. A parent who refuses tracking apps may be judged as neglectful. A tenant who resists installing smart devices may be considered difficult. The very act of resistance is reframed as irrational, paranoid, or irresponsible. When surveillance becomes common sense, disobedience appears deviant not to the state or corporation alone but to peers, colleagues, and communities. *The power of contemporary systems lies not in forcing compliance but in making compliance indistinguishable from normalcy.*

This chapter traces how obedience is manufactured not through dramatic confrontations with authority but through the routines of daily life. By examining the technologies of workplace monitoring, the integration of smart homes, the parental embrace of tracking, and the broader cultural acceptance of ordinary control, it becomes clear that the infrastructure of surveillance does not rely on spectacular displays of force. Instead, it depends on its ability to appear harmless, efficient, and benevolent. The deeper danger is not that individuals are coerced but that they stop perceiving obedience as obedience at all. What emerges is a culture in which control is internalised and resistance is redefined as excess, paranoia, or dysfunction. The lesson is unsettling but vital: obedience today is engineered most effectively not where people fear power but where they forget it is even being exercised.

Workplace Monitoring: Corporate Obedience Regimes

The office used to be a space of negotiated trust, where a manager's oversight was balanced by a worker's discretion, autonomy, and skill. That balance is eroding. The modern workplace is increasingly defined by monitoring technologies that record, analyse, and feed back every keystroke, every pause, and every biometric sign of fatigue or alertness. What was once supervision has mutated into datafication, where performance is not judged by tangible results alone but by streams of quantifiable signals that claim to capture productivity, loyalty, and even character. *The central shift is that the worker no longer simply does the job; the worker becomes the job's data.*

Employee tracking software sits at the heart of this new regime. Tools such as Hubstaff, Time Doctor, or Teramind promise employers "unprecedented visibility" into how employees use their time. Screenshots are captured every few minutes, mouse movements are logged, and idle minutes are flagged. For workers, the effect is a quiet but persistent awareness that their labour is not simply measured in outputs but in continuous digital presence. The productivity dashboard—ostensibly neutral and objective—reshapes behaviour more effectively than a manager's reprimand. Employees adapt not to do their best work, but to avoid the negative signals the system might record. Pauses for reflection or informal chats, once considered integral to creative and collaborative processes, now register as inefficiency. *Surveillance thus does not just observe productivity; it redefines it in ways that prioritise compliance with metrics over meaningful contribution.*

Biometric checks extend this logic into the physical body itself. Fingerprint scans, facial recognition log-ins, and wearable devices used to monitor fatigue or stress are no longer restricted to high-security environments. Logistics companies equip drivers with cameras that track eye movements to detect drowsiness; warehouses deploy wristbands to monitor hand movements, optimising speed and efficiency. These systems are justified in terms of safety or accuracy, but the deeper effect is disciplinary. They bind the worker's body to the rhythms of the machine and make deviation visible. *Biometric monitoring collapses the line between the personal and the professional: your body is no longer yours alone when its signals are continuously harvested as corporate data.*

For many employees, the experience is one of subtle internalisation. Once a dashboard or wearable dictates what "good performance" looks like, workers begin to self-correct, often pre-emptively. A warehouse worker may pick faster not because they are told to, but because their wristband vibrates when their pace dips. An office worker may avoid checking personal messages, not because a supervisor warned them, but because their keystroke log will record the lull. The power of these systems lies less in direct punishment than in the cultivation of a constant self-discipline. *This is obedience rendered efficient: the worker no longer requires external correction, because the system has installed correction within their own routines.*

Case studies highlight how far-reaching these dynamics have become. During the COVID-19 pandemic, the rapid shift to remote work was accompanied by an explosion in demand for digital monitoring tools. Companies sought to replicate the visibility they had lost when employees left the office. Software firms marketed "bossware" that not only logged hours but also used webcams to detect presence, prompting workers to remain at their desks even during breaks. Employees reported drinking less water or avoiding bathroom trips for fear of appearing idle. The irony was striking: a pandemic that made autonomy essential in many aspects of life also entrenched unprecedented levels of corporate surveillance. *Moments of crisis often accelerate, rather than challenge, the expansion of monitoring regimes.*

Supporters of workplace monitoring argue that such systems promote fairness and accountability. They claim that data-driven insights replace managerial bias, ensuring that promotions and evaluations are based on measurable performance rather than favouritism. From this perspective, workers benefit as much as employers. Yet the reality is more complex. Metrics often privilege quantity over quality, speed over thoughtfulness, and conformity over creativity. They rarely capture the nuances of collaboration, empathy, or innovation—qualities essential in many professions but invisible in keystroke logs or biometric readings. *When fairness is defined solely by what is measurable, entire dimensions of human work disappear from recognition, and the result is not justice but impoverishment of value.*

The implications extend beyond individual workplaces. As more companies adopt these tools, norms of constant visibility spill across sectors. What is tolerated in a warehouse may migrate into offices; what is normalised in corporate settings may influence schools or government agencies. Workers accustomed to dashboards and biometric checks carry those expectations into other parts of their lives, from fitness apps to online learning platforms. The corporate regime of obedience thus does not remain confined to the workplace; it becomes part of a broader culture of self-monitoring. *The workplace is not merely where surveillance is applied; it is where surveillance is normalised for society as a whole.*

Critics also point to the psychological toll of constant monitoring. Studies show that employees under surveillance report higher stress, reduced job satisfaction, and diminished trust in their employers. The paradox is that tools introduced to enhance productivity can erode the very conditions—trust, autonomy, creativity—that make sustained productivity possible. Moreover, workers often feel infantilised, stripped of the dignity of being treated as professionals capable of self-management. *Surveillance undermines the very reciprocity on which healthy work relations depend: trust is replaced by suspicion, and collaboration is replaced by compliance.*

Yet resistance is limited. Few employees are in a position to reject these systems outright, particularly in competitive labour markets where alternatives are scarce. Collective bargaining has weakened in many industries, reducing the capacity of workers to push back against intrusive technologies. And even when employees protest, companies frame monitoring as essential for security, efficiency, or fairness—values difficult to oppose without appearing irresponsible. Resistance often takes the form of minor evasions: employees finding ways to keep their devices "active" while resting, or creating informal communication channels beyond the reach of monitoring software. But such evasions rarely challenge the system itself; they merely provide temporary relief within it. *Obedience is not enforced by brute force but by narrowing the legitimacy of resistance.*

Ultimately, workplace monitoring represents more than an evolution in management practice; it embodies a cultural shift in the meaning of work itself. Labour is no longer judged primarily by output but by compliance with systems that claim to represent objective truth. Data is treated as more trustworthy than human judgement, even when the data is partial, context-blind, or misleading. Workers are compelled not just to perform tasks but to continually perform their productivity for the system that measures them. In this sense, the monitored workplace is not just a site of labour but a laboratory for obedience, where habits of self-discipline are cultivated, exported, and entrenched. *The logic of corporate surveillance is not limited to profit—it is the production of compliant subjects for a datafied society.*

Smart Homes, Smarter Masters

The modern home, once imagined as the ultimate sanctuary from public oversight, is increasingly porous. The walls that historically kept prying eyes out now conceal devices that watch, listen, and learn with a level of intimacy no employer, government, or stranger could previously achieve. Smart speakers, thermostats, doorbell cameras, and fitness-integrated appliances are marketed as instruments of convenience, efficiency, and personal empowerment. Yet beneath this promise lies a subtler reality: *these devices do not merely serve household routines, they shape them, bending behaviour to patterns that align with corporate interests and data extraction.* The smart home is thus not simply a site of comfort but a frontier where surveillance merges seamlessly with daily life, all under the banner of modern living.

Consider the smart speaker, perhaps the most emblematic device of this transformation. Amazon's Alexa or Google's Assistant are presented as helpful companions: ready to dim the lights, play music, or manage a shopping list with a single spoken command. But each request is also a data point, captured and stored to refine predictive models of human behaviour. These devices do not just record what we ask; they learn when we ask, how often, and in what context. Patterns of speech and preference accumulate into behavioural profiles that become immensely valuable for targeted advertising and service development. *In the act of asking Alexa to turn off the lights, the consumer trains a system that gradually learns how they live, sleep, and spend.* The home is no longer a private space but a sensor-rich environment feeding continuous information to external servers.

Smart thermostats tell a similar story. Marketed as tools for reducing energy bills and promoting environmental responsibility, they map when households are occupied, when people wake, when they sleep, and how comfortable they wish to feel at particular times of year. The thermostat learns patterns of presence and absence so precisely that it can infer work schedules, travel habits, or even periods of illness. This data extends far beyond climate control; it reveals rhythms of life that companies can use to design services, price insurance, or predict purchasing habits. *The efficiency narrative masks the deeper reality that such devices do not just follow the household—they train it into predictable, optimised patterns aligned with external incentives.*

The smart doorbell, with its embedded camera and cloud storage, introduces yet another layer. These devices are sold as tools of security, offering homeowners reassurance that they can monitor their property remotely. Yet the footage they collect often extends beyond the household itself, capturing neighbours, passers-by, and delivery workers in a continuous archive. Police departments in several countries have partnered with doorbell companies to gain access to footage, effectively extending the reach of law enforcement into private neighbourhoods. What begins as a personal security tool becomes part of a larger surveillance infrastructure, blurring the boundaries between corporate and state monitoring. *The home thus shifts from a private retreat into a node within a wider system of control, with the resident as both consumer and unwitting deputy in the policing of public space.*

Crucially, these technologies do not operate neutrally. They subtly reshape household routines by rewarding certain behaviours and discouraging others. The ease of voice commands makes it less likely that household members will question the accumulation of dependency on a single platform. Energy-saving suggestions from a thermostat may prompt families to align their schedules more rigidly with the device's recommendations. Children grow up in environments where speaking to machines is naturalised, and where constant monitoring is not exceptional but mundane. *What is sold as empowerment is in fact a form of conditioning: the household learns to live in ways that are compatible with the logic of data-driven optimisation.*

The framing of smart home technologies is critical to their acceptance. Advertising stresses safety, progress, and responsibility. A smart lock secures the family; a smart camera protects the children; a smart appliance conserves resources. These narratives deflect concerns about privacy or autonomy by situating the technology as a moral good. Resisting or rejecting such devices is subtly cast as irresponsible: why would one not want their family to be safer, their home greener, their life more efficient? *The rhetoric of care disguises the deeper reality of control, ensuring that surveillance enters the home not as an intruder but as a welcome guest.*

The economic model underlying these systems reveals their true orientation. Few smart home devices are sold as one-off purchases; instead, they are tied to ecosystems that encourage ongoing subscriptions, upgrades, and service dependencies. Consumers are enticed with convenience, but the real transaction is the continuous supply of behavioural data, which can be monetised many times over. This creates incentives not simply to monitor but to nudge: devices suggest purchases, subscriptions, or adjustments that benefit the provider. In effect, the home becomes a site of behavioural engineering, where everyday choices are subtly shaped to maximise engagement and spending. *The smart master does not merely observe; it cultivates patterns of obedience dressed as personal preference.*

Case studies reveal how deeply such systems can penetrate. In one example, insurers in the United States experimented with offering discounts to customers who installed smart thermostats, effectively turning a voluntary adoption into a financial incentive. In another, law enforcement agencies accessed smart speaker recordings during criminal investigations, raising questions about whether the private home can still be considered a safe space for candid conversation. In China, integration of smart home technologies with broader state-driven platforms illustrates how household data can become a component of social credit systems. The lessons are clear: once the infrastructure of surveillance is embedded in domestic spaces, its uses are limited less by technical capacity than by shifting political and economic will.

Philosophically, the transformation of the home carries profound implications. Historically, the household has been understood as a domain of intimacy, autonomy, and refuge from external power. The intrusion of smart technologies challenges this boundary. The distinction between private and public, intimate and institutional, collapses when one's daily routines are continuously mediated by systems designed for external benefit. *The home is no longer a retreat from the market or the state but a site where their logics are most deeply inscribed, precisely because they operate under the guise of comfort and care.*

Resistance to this encroachment is complicated. Few people are willing to forgo the convenience of voice commands or the security of networked cameras. Moreover, opting out increasingly marks individuals as unusual or even paranoid, reinforcing the sense that resistance is abnormal. As with workplace monitoring, the genius of smart home surveillance is that it requires little enforcement; compliance is secured through cultural normalisation and personal preference. People do not feel watched against their will; they participate willingly, often enthusiastically, in systems that monitor them precisely because these systems are entwined with routines of domestic life. *Obedience becomes banal, achieved not through coercion but through the naturalisation of convenience.*

The broader trajectory suggests that smart homes represent more than a technological upgrade. They are experimental environments where behavioural data can be harvested with unprecedented intimacy and where patterns of dependence can be shaped across generations. The lessons learned in the home radiate outward: children raised with smart devices accept continuous monitoring in schools; adults accustomed to algorithmic scheduling adapt easily to workplace dashboards; families that normalise cloud-stored security footage accept broader forms of data sharing. In this way, the smart home is not only a microcosm of surveillance society but also its training ground. *By consenting to be managed in private, individuals are prepared to be managed in public.*

What emerges from this analysis is that the promise of the smart home is inseparable from its risks. Convenience and control, efficiency and surveillance, security and dependency are intertwined. The devices that simplify domestic life are also instruments that redraw the boundaries of autonomy and reshape the very meaning of privacy. They are not neutral assistants but architects of behaviour, installed not only in our homes but in our routines, relationships, and expectations. *The smart home's true master is not the resident but the system itself, quietly engineering obedience under the guise of service.*

Parenting in the Age of Tracking

Childhood, once seen as a space of exploration, unpredictability, and occasional mischief, is increasingly subject to a level of scrutiny that rivals that of high-security workplaces. Parents today are presented with a growing arsenal of apps and devices that promise peace of mind: GPS trackers embedded in watches, apps that log a child's every movement in real time, dashboards that provide data on sleep, screen time, and even social interactions. These technologies are sold as tools of care and safety, yet their deeper consequence is the normalisation of a surveillance culture that begins at birth. *When children grow up being constantly observed, recorded, and measured, they internalise surveillance not as an intrusion but as a condition of ordinary life.*

The first wave of such monitoring often starts before a child can even speak. Baby monitors now come with internet connectivity, facial recognition, and biometric tracking that records sleep cycles, breathing patterns, and room temperature. What was once a simple audio device to alert parents if a child cried has transformed into a data-rich platform. Parents are reassured that they can "optimise" their baby's health with these insights, but the logic is clear: *the earliest stages of life are already folded into systems of measurement and comparison.* Data becomes the arbiter of good parenting, with mothers and fathers encouraged to rely less on intuition and more on metrics generated by a third-party platform.

As children grow, wearable trackers extend this logic. Smartwatches marketed to parents allow them to know a child's precise location at all times, communicate remotely, and receive alerts if the child leaves a designated "safe zone." While the marketing narrative emphasises protection against abduction or accidents, the devices function just as much as tools of behavioural control. A child who knows their movements are being tracked learns to regulate themselves in accordance with the invisible presence of surveillance. The lesson is absorbed early: privacy is conditional, trust is mediated by data, and independence must always be supervised. *Surveillance ceases to be extraordinary; it becomes the grammar of everyday childhood.*

Educational institutions amplify this trajectory. Schools increasingly adopt monitoring technologies such as RFID-enabled ID cards, biometric attendance systems, and learning analytics platforms that track everything from keystrokes to emotional engagement during online classes. Parents are reassured that such tools promote safety and academic excellence. Yet the effect is to create a generation for whom being tracked, logged, and analysed is inseparable from learning itself. The child does not merely study under the gaze of a teacher; they study under the persistent gaze of systems designed to record and evaluate them continuously. *Schooling and surveillance intertwine so tightly that one becomes indistinguishable from the other.*

Parental motivations are not malicious. The appeal of tracking is deeply tied to legitimate anxieties about safety, particularly in urban contexts where dangers—real or exaggerated—loom large. The fear of letting children roam unsupervised, once considered a normal part of childhood, is now framed as neglect. Apps that provide real-time reassurance seem like responsible tools for modern parenting. But in protecting children from external risks, these systems create a different kind of risk: *they prepare young people to accept monitoring as an unquestioned condition of adult life.* The very technologies meant to safeguard childhood also diminish it by stripping away spaces of autonomy, secrecy, and experimentation.

The commercial interests behind these tools are significant. Tracking apps generate revenue not only through subscription fees but also through the sale of aggregated behavioural data. Information about how children move, what they consume, and how they sleep is valuable to advertisers and insurers. Tech companies frame these tools as neutral instruments of care, but their economic model depends on habituating both parents and children to the idea that intimate behavioural data should be collected, stored, and analysed. The result is a family life that subtly reorganises itself around metrics and notifications, where trust is measured not in relationships but in data streams. *Parental love becomes entangled with corporate interests, producing a home environment where surveillance is both emotional reassurance and commercial transaction.*

Case studies highlight this entanglement. In the United States, certain parental control apps gained notoriety for quietly sharing location data with third-party brokers, selling it to advertisers or even law enforcement. In China, education apps widely used in schools feed data into centralised systems that can influence student rankings and opportunities. In Europe, legal controversies have emerged over whether child-tracking apps comply with data protection laws such as GDPR, revealing how deeply these technologies test the limits of privacy frameworks. What unites these cases is the way surveillance infrastructures, once introduced for parental reassurance, evolve into platforms with uses and consequences far beyond their original promise.

Philosophically, the implications are profound. Childhood has long been understood as a stage where autonomy and identity are gradually negotiated. Secret diaries, unsupervised play, and unmonitored friendships provided spaces where children tested boundaries and discovered themselves without oversight. Digital tracking technologies compress these spaces. When every movement can be traced, the conditions for secrecy and unobserved growth are eroded. *Surveillance transforms not only how children are parented but how they learn to inhabit themselves.* They are raised to be transparent subjects, accustomed to external verification rather than private reflection.

This normalisation of surveillance does not end with childhood. Adults who grew up being tracked by parents and schools adapt more readily to workplace monitoring, corporate productivity dashboards, or the invasive convenience of smart devices in their homes. The leap from a parent watching over you via an app to an employer monitoring your keystrokes feels less like an intrusion and more like continuity. The conditioning is subtle but powerful: *what begins as reassurance in childhood becomes obedience in adulthood.*

The ethical tension is sharp. Parents face real dangers in the world and cannot be faulted for seeking tools that promise to protect their children. Yet the reliance on tracking technologies shifts the balance between care and control. It teaches both parent and child that the ultimate guarantor of safety is surveillance, not trust, community, or resilience. In doing so, it diminishes the possibility of raising children who are comfortable navigating risk, making decisions independently, or cultivating responsibility without constant oversight. The paradox is stark: *in trying to raise safer children, we may be raising less free ones.*

Ultimately, parenting in the age of tracking illustrates how surveillance embeds itself not by force but by love. Parents adopt these technologies not because they wish to control their children harshly, but because they wish to care for them responsibly. Yet love becomes a vector for normalising systems that gradually erode privacy and autonomy. This is the subtle genius of surveillance: it cloaks itself in the most intimate human relationships, transforming affection into infrastructure. *The child learns early that to be loved is to be watched—and in learning this, they inherit a world where obedience to surveillance feels not imposed but natural.*

The Banality of Control

Control does not always arrive with the heavy hand of authority or the spectacle of surveillance cameras. More often, it seeps into daily life through unremarkable routines and conveniences that rarely invite scrutiny. It is in the loyalty card at the supermarket, the swipe of a transport pass, the default settings of a smartphone app. These systems are not dramatic; they are ordinary, even dull. Yet precisely because they are so banal, they exert a quiet but profound influence over how people behave, making obedience feel like common sense and resistance appear eccentric, paranoid, or needlessly confrontational. *Power today thrives not by displaying itself, but by embedding itself invisibly in the rhythms of everyday existence.*

Consider the workplace. Employee monitoring systems are no longer presented as instruments of surveillance but as productivity enhancers. A dashboard that tracks keystrokes or login hours is framed as a neutral tool for efficiency, something as mundane as a spreadsheet. Few workers openly resist because the practice is routinised; to protest seems out of proportion, a dramatic reaction to what is portrayed as a simple management aid. The result is compliance by default. Employees internalise the logic that efficiency requires oversight, and oversight requires data. The act of being monitored becomes as natural as filling out a timesheet, stripping it of the aura of intrusion that might otherwise provoke outrage.

The same logic extends into consumer life. Supermarket loyalty cards, ostensibly harmless tools for discounts, track purchasing patterns with extraordinary granularity. Customers trade privacy for small financial perks without perceiving it as a loss. The act of swiping a card is so mundane that it resists critical reflection. To question it—to refuse to participate—is to place oneself outside the flow of ordinary shopping, an act that risks appearing pedantic or paranoid. *What makes such systems powerful is not their overt coercion but their ability to render surveillance indistinguishable from routine transaction.*

Domestic life, too, has absorbed this banality of control. Smart speakers and thermostats promise convenience, tailoring music, lighting, or temperature to individual preferences. Yet every interaction feeds behavioural data back to corporations, refining predictive algorithms. The household, historically a private space, becomes a site of constant data extraction. Still, because these systems present themselves as helpers—obedient servants at the command of their owners—the relationship inverts. The user obeys by feeding data, while believing themselves in control. To resist adopting such devices often requires explaining one's refusal to others, making the sceptic appear reactionary, distrustful, or eccentric in a world where "everyone" already uses them.

Social norms amplify this perception. When surveillance becomes woven into collective life, resistance does not simply mean opting out; it means diverging from what is now considered normal. Parents who decline to install tracking apps on their children's phones may be judged as negligent. Workers who object to productivity monitoring may be seen as hiding laziness. Citizens who cover their webcams or avoid social media risk being labelled paranoid or antisocial. *The genius of banal control is that it enlists social pressure to discipline dissent, making the cost of refusal not just institutional but interpersonal.*

This is not accidental. Systems of control function best when they minimise friction and cloak themselves in the language of neutrality. A surveillance apparatus that feels extraordinary invites suspicion; one that feels ordinary is self-sustaining. Philosopher Michel Foucault described how modern power operates not through spectacle but through diffuse discipline, shaping conduct quietly and persistently. The banality of control exemplifies this: there is no centralised order commanding obedience, but countless small mechanisms—policies, apps, defaults—that make compliance feel like the path of least resistance. Resistance, by contrast, feels disruptive, uncomfortable, and excessive.

Real-world examples abound. In many cities, cashless public transport systems make it nearly impossible to travel without leaving a digital trace. Facial recognition at airports is presented as a way to speed up queues, not as a surveillance expansion. Health insurance apps encourage users to log steps, meals, and sleep habits, offering lower premiums in exchange for constant data-sharing. Each case illustrates how surveillance is bundled with convenience, efficiency, or savings. The exchange seems rational, even beneficial. Yet the cumulative effect is the transformation of ordinary life into a data-generating routine where obedience is embedded not through threat, but through habit.

Philosophically, this raises the problem of how freedom is experienced. Many imagine freedom as the ability to choose without coercion, but banal systems of control reconfigure the terrain of choice itself. When default options track users, when participation in basic services demands data disclosure, and when refusal carries social or financial costs, freedom contracts without any single moment of force. *The individual feels free in the act of choosing while the system ensures that most choices lead back to compliance.* The subtlety is what makes the system resilient: the absence of visible oppression masks the presence of structural control.

Resistance under these conditions becomes psychologically taxing. To resist is not simply to say no to an authority; it is to stand apart from routines that appear harmless. The dissenter must justify their scepticism constantly—why not use the app everyone else uses, why not take the discount, why not make things easier? The burden of proof shifts. It is no longer the system that must explain itself; it is the individual who refuses who must defend their choice. This inversion makes obedience the default and dissent the anomaly.

The implications are profound for democratic life. Surveillance states of the past relied on visible mechanisms of control—secret police, files, interrogations—that could be resisted through solidarity or exposure. Today's banal control disperses itself so widely and embeds itself so deeply in ordinary contexts that collective resistance becomes fragmented and rare. Citizens may recognise surveillance in theory but fail to perceive it as urgent in practice because it is everywhere and nowhere, diffuse and unremarkable. *Banality is not the absence of power; it is its camouflage.*

The banality of control thus represents the most insidious form of obedience. It does not provoke outrage, because outrage feels disproportionate to the stimulus. It does not incite mass resistance, because resistance seems eccentric against the backdrop of ordinary life. It works not by crushing dissent but by making dissent implausible, even embarrassing. And in this subtle transformation of perception lies its triumph: power that hides in banality requires no force to be obeyed, because it convinces its subjects that they are not obeying at all.

Chapter 10

The Global Convergence

Surveillance was once imagined as the defining mark of authoritarianism, an instrument of social control deployed by regimes fearful of dissent. Liberal democracies, by contrast, were meant to distinguish themselves through transparency, legal restraint, and respect for privacy. Yet the reality of the twenty-first century reveals a disquieting collapse of these boundaries. States that pride themselves on freedom have adopted techniques of monitoring, filtering, and behavioural prediction pioneered by governments they once criticised. Authoritarian regimes, for their part, have learned to refine and repackage their tools in ways that make them appealing and exportable, allowing techniques of digital control to flow across borders like capital or culture. *The convergence is not theoretical; it is already here, shaping the infrastructure of everyday life in ways that transcend ideology.*

This convergence is fuelled by at least three dynamics that reinforce one another. First is *authoritarian learning*: states study each other's methods, observe what succeeds in quelling dissent or shaping public behaviour, and adapt those strategies to their own contexts. When China deploys facial recognition to manage public gatherings, when Russia perfects the art of online disinformation, or when Western security agencies develop predictive policing algorithms, the lesson is not confined to their borders. Other governments observe, imitate, and modify. The world's laboratories of control, whether in Moscow, Beijing, London, or Washington, produce blueprints for global emulation. No government wants to appear less capable of governing digital society than its rivals, and so the bar of what is permissible creeps ever higher.

The second driver is technological export. Surveillance tools are not confined to national boundaries; they are sold, licensed, and embedded into the infrastructures of other states. Israeli spyware such as Pegasus has enabled governments across continents to monitor journalists, opposition figures, and activists with a precision previously reserved for intelligence elites. Chinese companies supply cameras and AI-driven monitoring platforms not only to their own cities but to municipalities in Africa, Latin America, and Europe, often bundled as part of wider infrastructure projects. American platforms, while presented as consumer services, have become the backbone of global digital ecosystems, harvesting data that can be monetised commercially or accessed by states through legal and extralegal channels. *Surveillance has become a transnational commodity, marketed as security, convenience, or modernisation, but ultimately serving as a shared foundation for algorithmic obedience.*

The third dynamic is the creeping normalisation within democracies themselves. Practices once considered repressive have been reframed as pragmatic responses to modern threats—terrorism, pandemics, cybercrime, misinformation. Border agencies in liberal states now rely on biometric databases to screen travellers. Police departments use predictive analytics to decide where to deploy patrols. Intelligence agencies collect vast quantities of metadata on the justification of protecting national security. Each measure may be defended as temporary or narrowly focused, yet together they redraw the boundaries of what liberal democracies consider acceptable. The point is not that democracies have become identical to authoritarian regimes, but that they are increasingly indistinguishable in the techniques they deploy, differing mainly in the narratives they attach to their use.

The outcome is a shared digital order that transcends political systems. Authoritarian and democratic governments alike are converging on a logic where legitimacy rests on the ability to monitor populations in real time, predict behaviour, and intervene before dissent crystallises. Ideological justifications vary—national stability, consumer safety, efficiency, public health—but the underlying architecture is strikingly similar. Data is collected at scale, analysed by algorithms, and used to shape conduct in ways that bypass traditional processes of persuasion or law. *What unites these systems is not their political rhetoric but their technical rationality: the conviction that governance is best achieved through the continuous capture and manipulation of behavioural data.*

This chapter traces how convergence has unfolded and why it matters. It examines the ways authoritarian learning creates a global marketplace of control strategies, how surveillance technologies are exported and integrated into diverse societies, and how democracies increasingly justify practices that were once the hallmarks of repression. It situates these developments within a broader narrative: the slow but decisive shift toward a unified logic of algorithmic governance that is indifferent to ideology, tradition, or national boundary. For the reader, the stakes are clear. The future of freedom may not hinge on overt clashes between democracy and authoritarianism but on whether societies recognise and resist the subtle merging of their digital infrastructures into one system of obedience. *The challenge is not that surveillance is spreading from one part of the world to another; it is that it is becoming the world itself.*

Authoritarian Learning

One of the most striking dynamics of the digital age is not simply that states are developing new tools of control but that they are learning from one another with remarkable speed. Repression is no longer an isolated national practice; it is a global laboratory in which techniques are tested, refined, and exported. A crackdown in one part of the world becomes a playbook elsewhere, often within months. Authoritarian learning has turned repression into a transnational discipline, in which strategies migrate not only through covert collaboration but also through open emulation, commercial export, and the subtle exchange of legitimacy. *The outcome is a world where the boundaries between authoritarian and democratic governance blur—not because ideology has disappeared but because the logic of control is converging across systems.*

The Chinese state is perhaps the most visible practitioner of this model. Its experiment with the Social Credit System—combining financial data, criminal records, online behaviour, and even patterns of social association into a unified metric—has been studied far beyond China's borders. Few governments have adopted its full apparatus, but many have borrowed its underlying logic: that behaviour can be engineered through the promise of rewards and the threat of subtle penalties, all administered algorithmically. India's Aadhaar biometric identity programme, though framed in terms of welfare delivery rather than obedience, echoes the same centralisation of personal data into a single state-linked system. Across Africa, governments have purchased Chinese surveillance cameras with AI-driven recognition features, not only because they are affordable but because they embody a model of governance that promises visibility over large, complex populations. *What begins as a domestic experiment quickly becomes a template for others who see both its effectiveness and its profitability.*

This diffusion is not unidirectional from East to West. Western governments have pioneered many practices later absorbed by authoritarian regimes.

The United States' embrace of predictive policing software, initially marketed as a neutral tool for crime prevention, has been closely observed by governments keen to pre-empt dissent as well as crime. The Patriot Act's expansion of surveillance powers after 9/11 provided legal justifications that other states could cite in defence of their own security expansions. Britain's extensive use of CCTV cameras, once considered an outlier in Europe, helped normalise the idea that constant urban monitoring was both lawful and practical. These precedents weaken the rhetorical barrier between democracy and authoritarianism, allowing states like Turkey, Hungary, or Egypt to argue that their own intrusions are simply variations of accepted global practice. *When democracies expand surveillance, they inadvertently furnish authoritarian regimes with cover.*

The exchange is also facilitated by private actors. Authoritarian learning does not always require governments to negotiate directly; it can be outsourced to corporations that provide the tools. Israeli spyware such as Pegasus demonstrates how small, technologically advanced states can project influence by selling highly intrusive tools to governments across the globe, from Mexico to Morocco to Saudi Arabia. Chinese firms like Hikvision and Dahua provide surveillance infrastructure under the banner of "safe cities," often bundled into development aid or infrastructure projects. American companies, while often presented as consumer-facing platforms, play a subtler role by exporting the infrastructure of data extraction and behavioural profiling that governments then appropriate. Facebook's Free Basics initiative in developing countries, ostensibly about providing internet access, created ecosystems where data flowed freely to a private American corporation but could also be tapped by local states. *Commercial exchange ensures that even governments with limited technical capacity can rapidly adopt sophisticated control mechanisms.*

What makes this process so potent is not merely the circulation of technology but the circulation of justifications. Every repressive measure is framed in terms that travel well: security, stability, economic development, public health. When China deploys facial recognition to manage public gatherings, it speaks the language of safety and efficiency. When Britain rolls out data-driven counter-terrorism programmes, it emphasises prevention and proportionality. When France introduces stricter online hate-speech laws, it invokes the defence of democracy itself. These narratives cross borders as readily as the tools themselves, offering states a menu of rationales that sanitise intrusion. *The language of necessity becomes as exportable as the hardware and software of surveillance.*

At the same time, authoritarian learning is not seamless imitation. Governments adapt foreign strategies to their own political cultures and institutional frameworks. In Singapore, behavioural nudging and urban monitoring have been embedded into a broader narrative of technocratic governance, cultivating acceptance rather than fear. In Russia, by contrast, control has taken a more aggressive form, blending digital repression with physical coercion and disinformation. The United Arab Emirates has fused Western-style consumer data profiling with authoritarian political controls, building a model where shopping malls and state security coexist within a single infrastructure of tracking. Each adaptation underscores a larger truth: *the mechanics of digital control are modular, capable of being reassembled to suit vastly different political projects.*

The consequences of this transnational borrowing are profound. First, it erodes the possibility of isolating or sanctioning authoritarian practices. If predictive policing is used in Los Angeles as well as Lagos, or if biometric databases exist in both India and China, how can one draw a principled line against their global spread? Second, it accelerates the pace of innovation in repression. Each government does not have to start from scratch; it can learn from the successes and failures of others. The violent dispersal of protests in Hong Kong taught governments elsewhere how to blend physical policing with digital incapacitation, while the failure of Egypt's internet blackout during the Arab Spring demonstrated the risks of crude shutdowns, leading to more sophisticated throttling techniques in later uprisings. *The global circulation of tactics makes resistance more difficult because authorities are already studying and adapting to past failures.*

Finally, authoritarian learning creates a paradoxical form of internationalism. While states may clash ideologically or economically, they are remarkably aligned in their willingness to adopt digital tools that entrench their authority. China and the United States may contest for technological supremacy, yet their respective surveillance practices reveal a shared conviction: that data is the substrate of governance and that visibility over populations is indispensable. This convergence does not erase ideological differences, but it ensures that, at the level of technical infrastructure, governments increasingly resemble one another. *The shared grammar of control is becoming more durable than the divisions of political rhetoric.*

To understand contemporary governance, then, is to recognise that repression is no longer contained by borders. Authoritarian learning means that a protest in one city, a policy in one parliament, or a technology deployed in one authoritarian stronghold can echo worldwide. The digital era has transformed authoritarianism into a global commons—not of liberty but of control—where every experiment is an export and every refinement a lesson to others. What distinguishes our age is not simply the existence of surveillance but the speed with which it travels, adapts, and legitimises itself across political systems. *The world is not witnessing isolated pockets of authoritarianism but the emergence of a shared toolkit of obedience, assembled collectively by states that, despite their differences, have learned to converge on the same logic of control.*

The Export of Surveillance Tech

Surveillance technology is no longer bound to the political geographies that birthed it; it is a global commodity, exported, licensed, and embedded across borders with the efficiency of any other industrial product. What was once the exclusive domain of secret police and intelligence agencies is now manufactured, branded, and shipped internationally, often through channels as mundane as development aid packages, law-enforcement exchanges, or private procurement contracts. *The tools of digital control are not confined to authoritarian states but circulate widely, shaping governance across democracies, semi-democracies, and outright dictatorships alike.*

Israel's Pegasus spyware has become a defining symbol of this globalisation. Developed by NSO Group, Pegasus can infiltrate smartphones silently, granting operators the ability to read messages, track locations, and activate microphones without the user's knowledge. It has been sold to governments across the Middle East, Africa, Europe, and Latin America, officially under the justification of counter-terrorism and crime prevention. Yet investigative reports have shown that Pegasus has been used against journalists, activists, opposition politicians, and even heads of state. What is striking is not only the software's technical sophistication but its portability: it allows states with limited cyber capabilities to instantly acquire world-class intrusion powers. In effect, *a government does not need its own NSA if it can simply buy one off the shelf.* Pegasus illustrates how surveillance technology functions as a force multiplier, enabling regimes of varying strength to leapfrog their developmental constraints and enter the league of advanced digital control.

China's role in exporting surveillance is no less significant, though it is anchored less in spyware than in physical infrastructure. Companies like Hikvision and Dahua dominate the global market in networked cameras, many with built-in facial recognition and AI-driven tracking. These systems are marketed under the branding of "safe cities" or "smart cities," framing their adoption as modernisation rather than repression. From Ecuador to Kenya to Serbia, governments have installed Chinese-built monitoring systems as part of urban management projects. In practice, the cameras extend state visibility into everyday life, often linked to centralised command centres. The political implications are twofold. First, they offer states the capacity to monitor dissent as easily as traffic congestion. Second, they come bundled with political influence: many of these projects are financed through Chinese loans or included in Belt and Road Initiative agreements, tying surveillance adoption to broader economic dependence. *The export of Chinese surveillance hardware is thus inseparable from the export of its governance model—ubiquitous monitoring as a feature of order.*

American platforms represent a subtler but equally consequential form of surveillance export. Unlike Israeli spyware or Chinese cameras, which are marketed directly to governments, American technology giants export infrastructures of behavioural data collection under the guise of consumer convenience. Facebook, Google, Amazon, and Apple provide tools and services that have been adopted worldwide, embedding data-harvesting logics into everyday life. While these companies insist they do not sell directly to repressive governments, the ecosystems they create make surveillance easier. Facebook's platform, for example, has been leveraged by governments in Myanmar and the Philippines to monitor and manipulate citizens. Amazon's Ring doorbells and Alexa devices, promoted as lifestyle enhancements, have been integrated into police partnerships in US cities and exported abroad, creating networks of privately owned sensors feeding into state surveillance systems. *The export of American platforms demonstrates that surveillance does not need to arrive as a weapon; it can arrive as a lifestyle product and only later reveal its political implications.*

The convergence of these exports—Israeli intrusion, Chinese infrastructure, American platforms—creates a global marketplace where governments can select from a menu of capabilities. An African state concerned about urban unrest might purchase Chinese cameras for visibility, Israeli spyware for precision targeting of opposition leaders, and American social media analytics to track narratives online. A European democracy might implement the same tools under the justification of counter-terrorism, and the distinction between authoritarian and democratic use narrows to the thinnest line of rhetoric. *Surveillance technology, once exported, becomes ideologically neutral; it is the context of its use that determines whether it is called security or repression.*

This globalisation of surveillance also reshapes accountability. When abuses occur—when spyware is used against a journalist, or when cameras are deployed against peaceful protesters—the responsibility is diffused. The exporting company may claim it only licensed the tool for lawful use. The importing government may argue it acted within sovereign prerogatives. The platforms may insist their systems were "misused" by local actors. The result is a governance vacuum in which powerful tools of control circulate widely without effective oversight. This diffusion of accountability is not accidental; it is a feature of the way surveillance technology is commodified. *What makes the export of surveillance unique is that it generates global capabilities without generating global responsibilities.*

Philosophically, the export of surveillance represents a reversal of one of modernity's central assumptions: that technologies of governance evolve within specific political systems. In the past, methods of control—whether the Stasi's file drawers or Britain's colonial census—were rooted in national or imperial projects. Today, surveillance technologies are detached from their origins, flowing transnationally with the speed of software updates or shipping containers. This makes them harder to contest, for one cannot simply oppose a national policy when the same tool is available from multiple suppliers worldwide. Resistance must grapple with a decentralised ecosystem where surveillance is not a monopoly of any one power but the shared output of global industry. *Surveillance is no longer the tool of a regime; it is the product of a market.*

At the same time, the circulation of surveillance tech fosters unexpected alliances. Democracies concerned about Chinese influence may nevertheless purchase Israeli spyware. Authoritarian states seeking legitimacy may frame their adoption of American platforms as signs of modernity. Hybrid regimes that straddle both democratic and authoritarian features can pick and choose tools that serve their immediate priorities. This cross-pollination erodes the ideological fault lines that once divided governance models. *When repression and convenience are manufactured in the same global factories, the distinction between them is harder to sustain.*

The export of surveillance technology therefore signals more than just an arms trade; it marks the construction of a shared digital order. States that otherwise compete for influence are bound together by common infrastructures of control. Citizens across the world, regardless of whether they live under authoritarian or democratic rule, find themselves embedded in systems that watch, record, and predict their behaviour. What differs is the narrative overlay: one citizen is told it is for safety, another for modernisation, another for counter-terrorism. But the architecture is the same. *The global circulation of surveillance tech is producing not a clash of systems but their convergence, stitched together by the quiet flow of cameras, code, and contracts.*

When Democracies Borrow Authoritarian Tools

The line between authoritarianism and democracy has traditionally been marked by the limits each system places on state power. In theory, democracies constrain the government through laws, oversight, and cultural commitments to rights, while authoritarian regimes expand their capacity to intrude unchecked into private life. Yet this distinction has grown increasingly fragile. Liberal democracies, often with the best of intentions, are adopting practices once associated with authoritarian regimes, reframing them as necessary, proportionate, or temporary measures. *The paradox is that democracy's tools of protection can, when repurposed, become instruments of control almost indistinguishable from those of the systems it claims to oppose.*

The shift is most visible in the expansion of surveillance justified by security concerns. After the attacks of 11 September 2001, the United States implemented the Patriot Act, vastly increasing the powers of intelligence agencies to collect communications data, monitor financial transactions, and conduct searches with minimal judicial oversight. What was sold to the public as a response to an extraordinary emergency soon embedded itself into routine governance. European states followed with their own equivalents, often under the logic of harmonising security frameworks against terrorism. The justification was always rooted in the language of necessity: democracies had to defend themselves against non-state actors that exploited their openness. Yet in practice, the tools—mass data collection, secret watchlists, and indefinite detentions—mirrored the very practices Western governments once condemned in their adversaries. *Exceptional measures in democracies rarely remain exceptions; once normalised, they become precedents for further expansion.*

The COVID-19 pandemic offered another window into this process. Contact-tracing apps, mobility restrictions, and vaccine passports were rolled out across Europe, North America, and Asia as public health tools. Many of these drew directly on technologies perfected in more authoritarian contexts, such as China's health code system, which integrated QR-based passes with geolocation data to determine who could travel, work, or enter public spaces. In democratic states, the introduction of such measures was softened by appeals to solidarity and scientific necessity. Yet the mechanisms—tracking individuals in real time, limiting their movements, and conditioning access to services on digital compliance—were indistinguishable in form from authoritarian precedents. The crucial difference was rhetorical: in democracies, the tools were said to expire once the crisis passed. But even as formal restrictions lifted, many infrastructures remained in place, ready to be reactivated for future emergencies. *The technologies of control have a half-life that far outlasts the crisis that justifies them.*

Beyond emergencies, democracies increasingly adopt authoritarian-style tools for everyday governance. Predictive policing algorithms, widely deployed in American cities, aggregate crime statistics and social data to direct police patrols. They are marketed as rational and objective, yet in practice they reproduce existing biases, concentrating surveillance and enforcement in already marginalised communities. In the United Kingdom, facial recognition trials have been justified as tools for public safety at events, echoing the Chinese state's defence of its own systems. Even in liberal democracies, biometric databases for immigration control now resemble the registries once associated with authoritarian management of populations. India's Aadhaar system, though not strictly authoritarian, is an illustrative example: the largest biometric database in the world, it was designed for welfare delivery but is increasingly used for authentication in both public and private life, raising concerns about mission creep and state overreach. *When democracies borrow authoritarian tools, they often wrap them in narratives of efficiency or fairness, but the effect—greater dependence on surveillance—remains.*

One reason democracies adopt such practices is the globalisation of technological standards. Tools developed in authoritarian contexts do not stay confined; they are marketed, exported, and adapted worldwide. As Chinese firms sell camera systems and Israeli companies license spyware, democracies purchase them under the same contracts as less free states. In doing so, they inherit not just the technology but the governance models embedded within it. A democracy may insist it uses facial recognition differently than China, but the architecture—the capacity to track individuals continuously—does not change. What shifts is the justification: in one case, it is national security; in another, counter-terrorism; in a third, preventing hooliganism at football matches. *The universality of the tool erodes the distinctiveness of the political system.*

Critics argue that democracies maintain a safeguard absent in authoritarian regimes: independent courts, free press, and electoral accountability. Yet these checks have limits when the technologies at stake operate invisibly and are legitimised under bipartisan consensus. Courts may rule against particular abuses, but they rarely dismantle entire systems once they are embedded. Citizens may vote, but elections seldom hinge on questions of surveillance infrastructure. Moreover, the complexity of the technologies themselves means oversight bodies often rely on the very agencies they are meant to regulate for technical expertise. *The opacity of algorithmic tools weakens the very mechanisms of democratic accountability that are supposed to restrain them.*

The danger is not that democracies will suddenly collapse into authoritarian states, but that they will incrementally hollow themselves out by adopting measures that erode civil liberties while preserving the appearance of normalcy. A citizen monitored by predictive algorithms, tracked by biometric databases, and nudged by behavioural platforms may still cast a ballot, but the substantive freedoms of association, privacy, and dissent are quietly diminished. This is why authoritarian borrowing is so insidious: it does not announce itself as repression but as pragmatism, modernisation, or even compassion. It tells citizens they are being cared for while silently extending the state's reach into their daily lives.

The longer-term consequence is a global convergence in governance practices. Democracies and authoritarian states alike are building on the same infrastructures of control, differing only in how they narrate them to their populations. When an authoritarian state claims that surveillance protects stability, and a democracy claims it protects safety, the functional outcome is nearly identical: citizens live under systems that watch, record, and regulate their behaviour. *The democratic distinction, once grounded in substantive limits on power, risks becoming little more than a difference in branding.*

If democracies are to avoid erasing the very values they claim to defend, they must grapple honestly with the fact that borrowing authoritarian tools cannot be justified indefinitely as temporary or exceptional. The challenge lies not only in resisting the temptation to adopt such measures, but in dismantling the infrastructures once they have been installed—a far harder task. For once tools of control become woven into the fabric of governance, they generate their own logic of indispensability. The risk is not that democracies will one day wake up as dictatorships, but that they will gradually stop noticing the difference.

Toward a Shared Digital Order

Power in the twenty-first century is increasingly exercised not through flags, armies, or constitutions, but through the quiet ubiquity of algorithms. What was once a matter of ideological contest—whether a society leaned democratic, socialist, or authoritarian—is gradually being reframed through a shared technical logic. The same recommendation systems that funnel citizens in China toward compliant behaviour on domestic platforms also shape consumer habits and political discourse in the United States or Europe. Surveillance infrastructures that grew out of authoritarian anxieties are now mirrored in liberal democracies under the language of efficiency, innovation, or safety. *The defining characteristic of the digital order is not that it differs across political systems, but that it converges around the same architecture of algorithmic obedience.*

This convergence is easiest to see in the global spread of social media platforms. Whether one lives under a one-party state or a parliamentary democracy, daily experience is increasingly mediated by platforms whose algorithms are optimised not for civic values but for engagement, retention, and prediction. These platforms train users to adapt to the rules of their feeds: to maximise visibility by tailoring expression, to regulate dissent through self-censorship when the algorithm penalises certain content, and to align with the metrics of likes, shares, or amplification. Here, ideology fades into the background. A citizen scrolling TikTok in Beijing and a teenager browsing TikTok in London participate in parallel systems of behavioural nudging, even if the political boundaries that govern what content is permissible differ. The point is not uniformity of censorship but uniformity of behavioural conditioning: the subtle training of individuals to align their actions with opaque systems of calculation.

Governments across the spectrum have noticed this disciplining power and have begun to integrate it into governance. Authoritarian states see platforms as tools of overt surveillance and censorship, while democracies increasingly deploy them as instruments of soft regulation. Content moderation policies, for instance, may be justified in democracies as a way to limit disinformation or hate speech, but the underlying mechanism—delegating authority to algorithms that silently prioritise some forms of expression over others—echoes the logics of control elsewhere. *The danger is that while justifications vary, the mechanics are converging: the reliance on automated systems to structure the limits of acceptable behaviour.*

The export of surveillance technologies has accelerated this convergence. Israeli spyware such as Pegasus has been sold to governments worldwide, from Mexico to India, enabling forms of targeted surveillance once available only to the most resource-rich intelligence agencies. Chinese firms dominate the global market for camera networks, equipping cities from Nairobi to Belgrade with the same facial recognition systems deployed domestically. American cloud service providers underpin the world's largest data infrastructures, ensuring that data collected in one jurisdiction is processed and monetised within frameworks developed elsewhere. The result is a planetary network of overlapping infrastructures where the origins of the technology matter less than the shared outcome: *citizens live under systems that are interoperable, transnational, and increasingly detached from national ideology.*

Even when democracies seek to regulate, they often end up reinforcing the shared order rather than breaking from it. The European Union's General Data Protection Regulation (GDPR) was designed as a rights-based framework, but in practice it entrenched the dominance of large platforms best equipped to comply with its requirements. Smaller competitors struggled with compliance costs, consolidating power in the hands of giants like Google, Meta, and Amazon. Similarly, proposals for AI regulation emphasise risk-based categories that assume the inevitability of algorithmic systems rather than questioning their proliferation. This reflects a broader tendency: even as democracies resist certain authoritarian excesses, they rarely challenge the underlying reliance on algorithmic mediation itself. *The shared digital order is sustained less by coercion than by consensus that such systems are indispensable.*

Critically, the convergence is not only technological but psychological. Citizens in vastly different political contexts are being habituated to the idea that constant monitoring, data exchange, and algorithmic ranking are normal. Workplace dashboards that measure productivity, health apps that track steps and sleep, and home assistants that listen for commands all cultivate the expectation that to live is to be measured. In China, this logic manifests in the social credit system; in the West, it appears in credit scores, insurance premiums tied to wearable data, or employee performance reviews extracted from keystroke logs. The contexts differ, but the underlying lesson is the same: obedience is not extracted by force but by participating in systems where compliance is rewarded with convenience, efficiency, and inclusion, while resistance leads to friction, exclusion, or invisibility.

The unifying feature of this order is the feedback loop. Unlike historical systems of surveillance, which relied on delayed processing—files, reports, and manual analysis—digital infrastructures provide real-time feedback. A protest flagged on social media can be suppressed in hours; a financial transaction deemed suspicious can be frozen instantly; a post outside the bounds of moderation disappears in seconds. The speed collapses the distinction between observation and response, producing a world where control is continuous and adaptive. What emerges is a *cybernetic form of governance*, in which human behaviour is not merely monitored but constantly steered by instantaneous signals.

This raises a profound philosophical question: if democracies and authoritarian states alike rely on algorithmic obedience, what differentiates them? Some argue that the difference lies in intent—that democracies use these tools to preserve freedom while authoritarian states use them to crush it. But intent may matter less than the lived experience of the citizen. A worker whose productivity is algorithmically tracked, a consumer whose choices are relentlessly shaped by recommendation engines, or a traveller whose biometric data determines access to borders may not care whether the system is operated by a democracy or an autocracy. What matters is the sense of constraint, the narrowing of unpredictability in daily life. *Ideology becomes secondary to infrastructure; the lived experience of control is converging across political divides.*

Yet the story is not one of simple homogenisation. There remain variations in how systems are deployed, resisted, or contested. In some democracies, civil society organisations challenge algorithmic excesses; in others, judicial rulings place limits on surveillance. Authoritarian regimes, for their part, often push their technologies to extremes, revealing more clearly the potential futures others may inherit. Still, the trajectory points toward alignment: the more nations borrow from each other's playbooks, the harder it becomes to maintain sharp distinctions. Democracies cite the security successes of authoritarian states to justify stronger surveillance, while authoritarian states adopt the language of efficiency and innovation pioneered in democracies to legitimise their own practices. The flow of ideas and tools goes both ways, binding states into a shared architecture of governance.

If there is a defining feature of this emerging digital order, it is not that it reflects the values of any single ideology, but that it erodes ideological distinctions altogether. The logics of visibility, data extraction, and feedback-driven compliance function as a kind of meta-politics—rules of the game that operate regardless of whether the players call themselves democratic or authoritarian. This order does not declare itself with manifestos or constitutions; it advances through standards, protocols, and defaults. It is stabilised less by force than by interoperability: a world in which platforms, sensors, and databases must be compatible across borders, and where citizens internalise the rhythms of algorithmic governance as part of ordinary life.

The pressing question, then, is not whether one belongs to a democracy or an autocracy, but how much of one's agency survives within a system designed to anticipate, shape, and pre-empt behaviour. *Algorithmic obedience is becoming the lingua franca of governance: a universal grammar of control that speaks across ideological divides.* What differs is not the structure of the sentence but the accent of its delivery—yet for those subject to its rules, the experience of being compelled to comply is strikingly familiar. The convergence is not a future to be speculated upon; it is already underway, quietly scripting the boundaries of freedom in the digital age.

Chapter 11

What Remains of Freedom

To speak of freedom in the twenty-first century is to step into a contested terrain. For much of modern history, freedom was imagined as autonomy from interference—the ability to live, think, and act without constraint. This vision was powerful, resonant, and politically mobilising. Yet it rested on a particular condition: that individuals could reasonably identify who or what was doing the constraining. The censor, the tyrant, the occupying power—each was a visible adversary against which freedom could be defined. In today's digital architectures, however, constraint is diffuse, algorithmic, and often invisible. What binds us are not overt prohibitions but the routines of platforms, the nudge of notifications, the efficiencies of data-driven convenience. The paradox of our age is that freedom still exists as a value, even as its substance is eroded by systems that discipline without declaring themselves as masters. To ask what remains of freedom, then, is not to pose a rhetorical lament but to confront the central philosophical and political question of the digital era.

Autonomy in this context cannot mean withdrawal from digital systems; such an exit is, for most, neither practical nor desirable. Instead, autonomy must be redefined as the capacity to navigate these systems with awareness, to understand the terms of participation, and to preserve spaces of unpredictability within infrastructures designed to anticipate and steer behaviour. *Freedom becomes less about rejecting systems outright and more about refusing to be fully scripted by them.* This shift demands intellectual humility: the recognition that the myth of total independence has always been just that, a myth. No society has existed without structures of constraint, but what marks the digital age as different is the depth of integration, the intimacy of the monitoring, and the speed of the feedback loops. Autonomy today is not the absence of constraint but the cultivation of agency within it—a capacity to see the levers, however small, that remain accessible.

These levers are not only theoretical but tangible. Across jurisdictions, citizens and governments have tested ways of reshaping the balance of power. Data rights legislation, from the European Union's GDPR to California's Consumer Privacy Act, has begun to formalise individual claims over information, forcing corporations to respond to demands for transparency or deletion. Civic campaigns—such as collective boycotts of platforms following scandals over data misuse—demonstrate that consumers can still exert pressure, even if such actions rarely dismantle underlying infrastructures. Political debates over algorithmic accountability, biometric regulation, and AI governance hint at possibilities for institutional intervention, though they are often reactive rather than anticipatory. These measures are imperfect, sometimes symbolic, and frequently co-opted. Yet their very existence proves that obedience is not absolute. *The cracks in the edifice remind us that systems, however pervasive, are neither eternal nor immune to contestation.*

Resistance, however, is not the exclusive domain of laws or movements. It also exists in the quiet, personal choices of individuals who refuse to fully capitulate to the logics of surveillance. The decision to use encryption, to block trackers, to opt out of invasive apps, or to compartmentalise digital identities may appear minor in the grand sweep of global data flows. Yet such acts matter precisely because they embody the refusal to normalise total visibility. They represent gestures of dignity, however fragile, and cultivate habits of critical engagement rather than passive submission. *What is at stake is not the fantasy of perfect invisibility but the preservation of margins where unpredictability survives.* Each act of resistance, however small, reminds us that freedom is not a singular event to be won or lost, but an ongoing practice.

To speak of freedom only in defensive terms, however, risks conceding too much ground. The deeper challenge is imaginative: to conceive of civic life that does not merely resist digital obedience but transcends it. Convenience has become the dominant moral currency of technological systems; platforms win legitimacy by offering frictionless experiences, faster transactions, and effortless connectivity. But if convenience becomes the ultimate horizon, freedom narrows to the choice of which platform's conveniences one prefers. A new civic imagination is required, one that asks whether efficiency should always trump unpredictability, whether speed should always override deliberation, and whether seamlessness should always eclipse privacy. This is not a call for nostalgia or regression, but for the revaluation of values in a world where technical systems increasingly dictate social rhythms.

Preserving unpredictability may prove to be the last defence of freedom. Surveillance systems thrive on prediction, on the capacity to map, anticipate, and pre-empt behaviour. To live in ways that are partially opaque to the system—to maintain unpredictability in thought, association, or action—is to preserve a space that cannot be fully domesticated by algorithms. This might take the form of supporting alternative platforms, cultivating analogue practices alongside digital ones, or insisting on deliberation in spaces where automation promises to decide for us. It might also require collective movements that prioritise values other than optimisation, creating institutions resilient to the seductions of efficiency. The point is not that unpredictability can abolish control but that it introduces friction, possibility, and plurality where systems seek closure.

The task, then, is not simply to identify what has been lost but to reclaim what remains. Freedom is not extinct, but it is fragile, contingent, and constantly renegotiated. It will not be restored by waiting for systems to collapse or for corporations to reform themselves. Nor will it be secured by isolated acts of refusal alone. What remains of freedom will depend on our willingness to redefine autonomy, to exercise the levers still at hand, to recognise the dignity of individual defiance, and above all, to imagine futures where life is not reducible to a predictable script of obedience. *The measure of freedom in the digital age may not be the absence of control but the persistence of unpredictability—the stubborn refusal of human life to be entirely captured by the logics of the machine.*

Redefining Autonomy in a Digital Age

Autonomy has long been one of the most celebrated principles of political and moral philosophy, often equated with independence, self-mastery, and freedom from coercion. In the Enlightenment tradition, autonomy was the hallmark of rational adulthood, distinguished from the dependency of childhood or the obedience of subjects to monarchs. To be autonomous was to stand alone, to think for oneself, to be governed by one's own reason rather than the will of others. Yet in the digital age, such a conception has become increasingly inadequate. The infrastructure of modern life is built upon systems so pervasive and interwoven that withdrawal from them is virtually impossible. To treat autonomy as independence is to misdiagnose the condition of our time. A more realistic and demanding understanding is required—one that frames autonomy not as absolute separation but as *conscious navigation within complex systems that cannot be abandoned without cost.*

Consider the everyday act of communication. To opt out of platforms such as WhatsApp, WeChat, or iMessage may be framed as an assertion of independence, but in practice it risks social exclusion. Friends, colleagues, and even civic services increasingly rely on these channels as default infrastructure. The "choice" to abstain can appear autonomous, but its consequence is isolation rather than empowerment. The lesson is not that autonomy has vanished, but that its form has changed. In environments where systems constitute the baseline for participation, autonomy becomes less about saying no and more about negotiating the conditions of yes. *The modern autonomous subject is not the solitary dissenter outside the system but the critical participant who understands the system's workings and adapts accordingly.*

This reframing demands a sober confrontation with the paradox of freedom in networked societies. On one hand, digital systems multiply opportunities for expression and connection. On the other, they discipline through subtle architectures of control—algorithms that nudge attention, interfaces that guide choice, and data economies that render individuals legible in ways they do not perceive. Autonomy here is not the fantasy of pure independence but the cultivation of literacy: the ability to see how environments shape behaviour, and to resist, redirect, or exploit those logics in ways that align with one's values. A user who understands the economics of attention can deploy ad-blockers, configure notifications, and cultivate habits of disconnection. They are not free from the system, but they have established a degree of agency within it. This is autonomy reimagined not as withdrawal but as tactical engagement.

The digital age also destabilises the boundary between individual autonomy and collective dependence. The lone figure asserting freedom against the system makes for powerful rhetoric, but in practice, autonomy often requires infrastructures of support. Encryption tools such as Signal exist not because individuals willed them into being but because communities of developers, activists, and funders collaborated to produce them. Data rights laws emerge not from singular acts of resistance but from collective mobilisation and political struggle. To exercise autonomy, therefore, is to participate in ecosystems that enable it. *Independence is a myth; interdependence is the reality. The question is not whether we rely on systems, but whether we shape or are shaped entirely by them.*

Philosophically, this shift aligns less with the Enlightenment ideal of the isolated rational actor and more with traditions that understand freedom as relational. The republican concept of non-domination, for instance, defines liberty not as the absence of interference but as protection against arbitrary power. Similarly, autonomy in a digital age might best be defined not as solitude from systems but as the ability to prevent those systems from exercising unchecked control. The right to data portability, the ability to challenge algorithmic decisions, or the choice to adopt privacy-enhancing tools all exemplify this approach. None eliminate dependency, but each introduces safeguards against domination. *Autonomy becomes a practice of conscious dependency—living within systems without surrendering entirely to their logic.*

Real-world examples illuminate both the promise and the fragility of this redefinition. In China, citizens have little practical choice but to use WeChat, an all-encompassing platform for messaging, payment, and official services. Yet within this constraint, some users creatively segment their online behaviour, maintaining parallel identities to preserve slivers of privacy. In Western democracies, where market competition ostensibly provides alternatives, the dominance of a handful of platforms produces similar dynamics. Opting for DuckDuckGo over Google, or Mastodon over Twitter/X, is an assertion of agency, but its efficacy is limited without broader adoption. These examples demonstrate both the possibility and the limitation of autonomy understood as navigation. It is neither total freedom nor total capture but a dynamic negotiation shaped by context.

There is also a psychological dimension to this shift. Autonomy has historically been linked to self-determination, yet algorithms increasingly anticipate and pre-empt desires before they are consciously articulated. Recommendation systems tell us what to watch, predictive text finishes our sentences, and health apps alert us before we notice our own symptoms. When choice is subtly pre-shaped, autonomy requires an additional layer of self-awareness: the recognition that decisions presented as natural may in fact be engineered. To be autonomous in this environment is to cultivate scepticism, to pause before accepting the defaults, and to interrogate whose interests those defaults serve. *Freedom lies not in rejecting tools of convenience but in refusing to conflate convenience with inevitability.*

One might object that this conception of autonomy risks diluting the term. If autonomy no longer means independence, is it not simply another word for coping? Yet this critique misses the point. The ideal of independence was always aspirational rather than literal. Even in pre-digital societies, autonomy was conditioned by economic necessity, social obligation, and cultural norms. What is distinctive today is not the fact of constraint but its form: algorithmic, predictive, and global in reach. To cling to independence as the benchmark is to guarantee despair; to redefine autonomy as conscious navigation is to preserve its relevance in a changed world. It is a humbler freedom, but one no less vital.

The stakes are profound. If autonomy is misdefined as independence, citizens may be paralysed by the impossibility of escape, retreating into cynicism or apathy. If, instead, autonomy is reconceived as navigation, then freedom remains practicable. The individual who deploys privacy tools, participates in civic campaigns, and develops digital literacy can still exercise meaningful choice. The community that demands data rights or challenges algorithmic opacity can still shift the trajectory of systems. Autonomy, in this sense, is not the heroic act of withdrawal but the persistent discipline of engagement. *To be free is not to stand outside the system but to refuse to be entirely determined by it.*

The challenge for the coming decades is whether societies can institutionalise this redefinition. Schools might teach algorithmic literacy alongside mathematics, cultivating citizens who can see through digital architectures of control. Governments might legislate to secure not only privacy but also the right to unpredictability, limiting the reach of predictive analytics into intimate domains. Civil society might invest in alternative infrastructures, from open-source software to cooperative platforms, that embody values other than extraction and optimisation. Each of these moves signals a recognition that autonomy is no longer an individual possession but a collective condition. Its preservation requires not only personal vigilance but structural design.

Ultimately, redefining autonomy in a digital age does not diminish its significance; it heightens it. The illusion of independence may have been comforting, but it was never sustainable in an interconnected world. By embracing autonomy as conscious navigation, societies acknowledge the inevitability of systems while insisting on the irreducible dignity of agency within them. This is not a concession but an evolution. Freedom has always been a practice rather than a possession. In the digital age, the practice must become sharper, more deliberate, and more aware of the architectures that seek to guide it. *Autonomy survives not by retreating from systems but by learning to move through them without surrendering the capacity to surprise, resist, and reimagine.*

Practical Levers of Resistance

It is easy to believe that resistance in the digital age is futile, that the scale of surveillance and the sophistication of algorithmic systems render individual or even collective defiance powerless. Yet history and contemporary politics suggest otherwise: while systems of control evolve, so too do the levers that can limit, redirect, or subvert them. The challenge is not that resistance is impossible, but that it requires new strategies, sharper forms of awareness, and a willingness to act collectively in ways that may at first seem incremental. *The most effective forms of resistance today are neither spectacular nor romantic; they are civic, political, and technological interventions that alter the architecture of power itself.*

The most significant lever in recent decades has come through law. The European Union's General Data Protection Regulation (GDPR), implemented in 2018, is frequently dismissed as an irritating pop-up exercise—the endless cookie banners that clutter online browsing. Yet behind this annoyance lies one of the most ambitious attempts to rein in corporate power over personal data. For the first time at scale, citizens were given enforceable rights: the right to access their data, to demand its deletion, and to know when it had been mishandled. Multinational companies, from social networks to e-commerce giants, were compelled to rethink their practices or face fines that reached into the billions. GDPR did not eliminate surveillance capitalism, but it established the principle that individuals' digital traces are not simply corporate property. *By codifying rights in law, it created friction against a model that thrives on frictionless extraction.*

Laws alone, however, are insufficient if they are not enforced or if they lag behind technological innovation. This is why civic mobilisation remains essential. The passage of GDPR itself was not a gift from above but the outcome of sustained campaigning by privacy advocates, consumer rights groups, and civil liberties organisations. More recently, movements such as "Stop Killer Robots," aimed at banning lethal autonomous weapons, show how global coalitions can set agendas even against powerful defence lobbies. In the United States, public outrage over the Cambridge Analytica scandal did not end data-driven politics, but it forced companies and regulators into debates that had long been avoided. Civic pressure rarely produces instant transformation, but it shifts the horizon of the possible. It ensures that resistance does not remain the province of lone dissidents but becomes the shared work of publics demanding accountability.

Collective economic action offers another lever. The mythology of the individual boycott—deleting one's Facebook account, refusing to use Amazon—often collapses under the reality of convenience and network effects. Yet collective boycotts, coordinated at scale, can alter corporate behaviour. In 2020, more than 1,000 companies, including major brands such as Unilever and Coca-Cola, temporarily withdrew advertising from Facebook in protest against its handling of hate speech. The campaign, "Stop Hate for Profit," did not fundamentally transform the platform, but it highlighted the vulnerability of surveillance-driven businesses to reputational and financial pressure. Similarly, consumer campaigns around sustainable technology—demanding fairer supply chains, longer-lasting devices, and repairability—illustrate how economic power can be wielded not by abandoning technology but by insisting that it align with broader values. *Resistance need not be rejection; it can also be redirection through economic leverage.*

Technological self-defence remains one of the most immediate and accessible forms of resistance. Encryption, once a niche tool for activists and journalists, has now become mainstream, embedded in everyday communication platforms from WhatsApp to iMessage. The spread of end-to-end encryption demonstrates that privacy-preserving technologies can reach mass adoption when designed for usability. Similarly, browser extensions that block trackers, search engines that do not profile users, and operating systems that prioritise privacy all represent ways in which individuals can reclaim some control. These tools are not perfect; metadata leaks persist, and corporations often co-opt privacy rhetoric for marketing purposes. But their existence is proof that technology can serve as a lever of resistance rather than only a mechanism of obedience. *Technological resistance succeeds when it scales, when it becomes the default rather than the exception.*

Yet the power of technological tools is inseparable from the political and legal frameworks that sustain them. Consider the battle over strong encryption. Governments in liberal democracies regularly argue that law enforcement requires "back doors" to encrypted services in order to combat terrorism and crime. Civil liberties advocates counter that any back door, once opened, becomes available to hostile actors, undermining the security of everyone. This is not a purely technical dispute; it is a struggle over whether privacy is a universal right or a conditional privilege. The outcome depends not only on code but on courts, legislatures, and public opinion. Thus, the lever of resistance is rarely singular; it is the interplay of technology, politics, and civic mobilisation that determines whether systems bend toward greater freedom or deeper control.

There are also less visible but equally powerful levers emerging through institutional resistance. Whistle-blowers, often at immense personal cost, have repeatedly revealed the scope of surveillance systems, from Edward Snowden's disclosures of the NSA's programmes to Frances Haugen's release of Facebook's internal research. Such acts do not dismantle the systems they expose, but they puncture the aura of inevitability. They provide the raw material for journalists, lawyers, and policymakers to build cases for reform. Resistance here is not about secrecy but about disclosure—about forcing systems designed to operate in obscurity into the light of public scrutiny. *Transparency, even when partial, remains a lever against systems that thrive on opacity.*

The digital age also allows for new forms of transnational resistance. Authoritarian learning, where states borrow techniques of digital control from one another, has been matched by activist learning, where movements share tactics across borders. From Hong Kong protesters using mesh networks to avoid detection, to European NGOs challenging the legality of facial recognition in courts, to African civil society organisations resisting imported surveillance technologies, resistance circulates globally. Each context differs, but the underlying insight is the same: the architecture of digital control is international, and so too must be the architecture of resistance. Levers that appear weak in isolation gain strength when they are linked across contexts.

Still, it is important to avoid romanticising these levers. Each is limited, partial, and vulnerable to co-option. Laws can be watered down or poorly enforced. Civic campaigns can lose momentum. Boycotts can be symbolic rather than transformative. Privacy tools can be absorbed into corporate ecosystems. Whistle-blowers can be silenced or ignored. The point is not that these levers are sufficient but that they exist, and that they matter. They complicate the narrative of inevitability that surveillance systems depend on. They remind citizens that obedience is not total, that systems of control can be bent, and that freedom remains contested terrain. *Resistance is not a singular act of defiance but an ongoing practice of pressure, adaptation, and creativity.*

What makes these levers compelling is not their capacity to restore an imagined past of total independence but their ability to carve out spaces of agency in the present. Data rights laws will not dismantle surveillance capitalism, but they force companies to reckon with citizen claims. Collective boycotts will not overturn monopolies, but they reveal vulnerabilities in corporate dependence on public legitimacy. Encryption will not prevent all forms of surveillance, but it raises the cost of intrusion. Each lever matters not because it delivers final victory but because it preserves the conditions under which autonomy remains possible. The task is not to dream of escape but to pull, persistently and strategically, on the levers that already exist.

To recognise these levers is to recognise the unfinished nature of digital systems themselves. They are not static architectures but evolving terrains, shaped as much by public contestation as by corporate design or state decree. Every law passed, every boycott staged, every technological tool developed, and every act of whistle-blowing shifts the balance, however slightly. Autonomy in the digital age does not reside in independence from these systems but in the capacity to engage them critically, to use the levers available, and to create new ones where none exist. *The freedom that remains is not the freedom of withdrawal but the freedom of resistance—and it is no less significant for being imperfect.*

Individual Acts of Defiance

The architecture of digital obedience is designed to make refusal seem either pointless or paranoid. Platforms and devices frame participation as inevitable, while the cost of opting out is social isolation, professional disadvantage, or sheer inconvenience. Yet even within this system of engineered compliance, individuals continue to carve out gestures of resistance. These gestures are rarely grand or revolutionary; instead, they are small, practical choices—encrypting a message, using privacy-focused tools, or refusing certain conveniences—that accumulate significance not because they dismantle surveillance but because they insist that agency has not entirely evaporated. *Acts of individual defiance matter less for their capacity to defeat the system than for their ability to keep alive the possibility of saying no.*

Encryption is one of the clearest examples of how a technical choice becomes a political act. To encrypt one's communications—whether through Signal, ProtonMail, or even WhatsApp's default end-to-end protocols—is to deny both states and corporations the easy visibility they presume. Governments have repeatedly sought to weaken encryption, often framing it as an obstacle to fighting terrorism, child exploitation, or organised crime. The "crypto wars" of the 1990s were thought to have ended when strong encryption became widely available, but similar debates persist in new forms today, as seen in the UK's Online Safety Act or the FBI's demands for "lawful access." Each attempt to mandate back doors exposes the deeper issue: encryption symbolises a refusal to trust power with unchecked access. *Using it is not paranoia; it is a rational assertion of the right to private speech in an environment where surveillance is the default.*

Privacy tools extend this form of everyday resistance beyond communications. Virtual Private Networks (VPNs), tracker-blocking browsers, search engines such as DuckDuckGo or Startpage, and open-source operating systems provide alternatives to the surveillance-heavy defaults of mainstream technology. These tools are often dismissed as niche, the domain of the technically literate or the ideologically committed. Yet their very existence demonstrates that the system is neither monolithic nor complete. Even when imperfect—VPNs can still leak data, private search engines still depend on broader infrastructures—they *change the texture of compliance.* They remind both users and providers that data extraction is not universally accepted, and they keep alive parallel infrastructures in which different values can be prioritised.

Lifestyle choices represent another, often underestimated, form of defiance. Choosing not to own a smart speaker, refusing to connect every device in the home, or deliberately minimising one's presence on dominant platforms are acts that resist the narrative of inevitability. Such choices are often derided as performative or futile, but their importance lies not in their direct impact on corporate profits but in their symbolic and cultural force. Every refusal signals that participation in the regime of total convenience is not compulsory. More significantly, these refusals demonstrate to others that opting out, even partially, remains possible. *Defiance becomes contagious when it is lived, not just theorised.*

Yet individual acts of resistance face a fundamental tension: they are both empowering and limited. Encrypting one's email does not halt bulk surveillance. Refusing a smart thermostat does not prevent the proliferation of smart cities. Abandoning Facebook does not disrupt the dominance of its advertising model. Critics argue, with justification, that such gestures amount to little more than self-protection for the privileged, or symbolic comfort for those who cannot alter structural conditions. But this critique overlooks the cumulative and pedagogical value of these acts. They may not dismantle the system, but they interrupt its claim to universality. They keep alive practices and infrastructures that might later be scaled, politicised, or collectivised. *The value of individual defiance lies less in what it achieves directly and more in what it preserves—the possibility of refusal in a system that thrives on inevitability.*

The history of resistance suggests that small gestures often seed larger transformations. The free software movement, once the preserve of eccentric programmers, laid the foundations for much of today's open-source ecosystem, from Linux servers to the Android operating system. What began as individual refusals to accept proprietary constraints became a global model of collaborative production. Similarly, early adopters of encrypted messaging paved the way for its eventual integration into mainstream platforms. The lesson is that acts of defiance scale unevenly but unpredictably, and their influence often exceeds the intentions of those who initiate them. To dismiss them as futile is to forget that systems are altered not only by frontal assaults but also by gradual erosions of legitimacy and by alternative practices gaining quiet traction.

At the same time, one must acknowledge the psychological dimension of individual resistance. For many, the act of encrypting a message or blocking a tracker provides not just functional protection but a sense of agency in a system designed to induce helplessness. This is not trivial. Power operates not only by extracting data but by convincing people that resistance is meaningless. Every individual gesture that refuses this fatalism reconstitutes the sense that one is still a subject capable of choice, however constrained. Philosophers from Hannah Arendt to Michel Foucault have emphasised that freedom often begins not with sweeping systemic change but with the assertion of capacity in the smallest of acts. *To resist is first to remember that resistance is possible.*

None of this is to romanticise individual defiance. It is unevenly distributed; those with resources, education, or technical literacy find it easier to adopt such tools and practices. Moreover, there is always the risk of commodification: "privacy" itself has become a marketing term, used to sell premium features or boutique devices while doing little to challenge the larger infrastructures of surveillance. But even this co-option reveals the persistence of demand. Companies sell privacy because enough individuals signal that they value it. The paradox is that individual resistance, even when absorbed into consumer markets, still shapes the discourse and forces concessions that would not otherwise exist.

The deeper importance of these acts is symbolic. A society in which nobody bothers with encryption, in which no one questions convenience, is a society in which obedience has become total. By contrast, a society where individuals routinely take small steps to shield themselves is one in which systems of control remain contested. The defiance may be incomplete, but it refuses closure. It ensures that the conversation about autonomy continues, that alternatives remain visible, and that the culture of compliance is never absolute.

In the end, individual acts of defiance should not be judged solely by their immediate efficacy but by their contribution to a longer horizon of resistance. They are reminders that power is not seamless, that cracks exist in even the most pervasive architectures of control. They are imperfect, fragile, and sometimes contradictory, but they are not meaningless. Each encrypted message, each refused device, each blocked tracker is a small but deliberate assertion that freedom is not yet entirely lost. *To live with defiance, however modest, is to refuse to let obedience be the only story told about life in the digital age.*

A New Civic Imagination

The most powerful feature of contemporary systems of control is not their brute force but their ability to disguise themselves as natural, inevitable, and convenient. The endless refinements of digital infrastructure have turned obedience into a background condition of daily life, rarely confronted directly because it is woven into ordinary routines. We do not experience ourselves as subjects of compulsion but as consumers making rational choices. This illusion is precisely what makes control effective. The question, then, is not only how to resist, but how to imagine living differently: what forms of collective life might break from the logic that equates efficiency with virtue, and convenience with progress? *Freedom today may depend less on breaking the system than on expanding the imagination of what life beyond algorithmic obedience could look like.*

To cultivate such a civic imagination requires recognising that predictability—so prized by both governments and corporations—is the enemy of liberty. Digital systems are designed to reduce uncertainty: platforms nudge our attention, logistics networks anticipate demand, predictive policing forecasts crime, and biometric checkpoints confirm identity with automated certainty. Unpredictability, once understood as a natural feature of human life, has come to be treated as a technical glitch or a security risk. Yet *the capacity for the unexpected is the foundation of democratic possibility*. If every action, preference, and movement can be modelled in advance, there is little space left for dissent, innovation, or surprise. The defence of freedom may therefore lie in preserving forms of unpredictability—spaces and practices where human life cannot be entirely captured by data.

This perspective reframes autonomy not as the solitary exercise of independence but as a shared condition. A person can encrypt their emails or refuse smart devices, but these gestures remain fragile without broader social infrastructures that recognise and support them. Laws that enshrine data rights, collective boycotts that challenge corporate practices, or community-driven networks that operate outside mainstream platforms—all are attempts to create a culture where individual refusals can flourish. *A civic imagination must move beyond the defensive posture of privacy towards the proactive creation of alternative norms and institutions.* In this sense, freedom is not only about protecting the individual but about reshaping the environment in which individuals act.

History offers a useful reminder that civic imagination has always been central to resisting domination. Nineteenth-century industrial workers did not simply ask for relief from exploitation; they imagined trade unions, cooperative enterprises, and universal suffrage. Civil rights movements did not only resist racial oppression but envisioned a world where equal dignity and participation were possible. These transformations were not inevitable; they were the product of communities daring to imagine forms of life that did not yet exist. Today's challenge is similar: to picture and construct ways of living with technology that do not collapse human freedom into consumer satisfaction or equate safety with surveillance.

One of the paradoxes of the digital age is that technologies which promise empowerment so often erode autonomy. Smart cities promise efficiency but diminish anonymity; platforms promise connection but extract behavioural data; algorithmic systems promise impartiality but encode bias. To respond only with critique is insufficient. A new civic imagination must propose alternatives. This does not mean utopian blueprints detached from reality but practical experiments in living differently: community-owned broadband networks, decentralised social platforms, open-source tools designed for transparency rather than extraction. These initiatives remain marginal, but they demonstrate that the current trajectory is not inevitable. *To defend freedom requires not just saying no to the dominant order but showing that yes—other ways are possible.*

Convenience, often treated as the ultimate good, must be re-examined. It is not that convenience is inherently corrosive, but that when it becomes the organising principle of society, it narrows the horizon of collective life. A culture that values convenience above all else will willingly trade unpredictability for comfort, oversight for efficiency, and obedience for seamlessness. A civic imagination must therefore embrace friction, uncertainty, and delay as conditions of freedom. The queue, the debate, the messy process of collective decision-making—these are not inefficiencies to be eradicated by algorithms but essential features of democratic life. *Freedom is not smooth; it is jagged, contested, and sometimes inconvenient.*

This insistence on unpredictability also reframes the role of art, culture, and public space. Authoritarian systems thrive on predictability not only in politics but in the imagination. Literature, theatre, protest, and art have historically disrupted the sense that the present order is permanent. In the digital age, the civic imagination must be nourished by spaces where people encounter ambiguity, contradiction, and surprise. These are the raw materials from which alternative futures are built. A society that eliminates unpredictability in the name of optimisation risks not only obedience but cultural impoverishment.

There is also a need to rethink solidarity. Resistance framed solely in terms of individual privacy risks becoming a luxury for the privileged, those with the time, resources, and technical skill to opt out. A civic imagination must instead foreground collective arrangements: public institutions that guarantee rights, civic technologies that prioritise communities, and solidarities that cross borders. After all, the infrastructures of control are global; surveillance technologies are exported, algorithms circulate across jurisdictions, and corporate platforms transcend nations. If freedom is to be defended, civic imagination must be similarly global, imagining solidarities that cut across the very borders that control seeks to harden.

The deepest challenge may be cultural: to shake off the fatalism that imagines digital obedience as a permanent condition. Power thrives when people believe there is no alternative. The civic imagination is therefore not a luxury but a necessity; it is what keeps alive the possibility that collective life can be organised differently. This requires courage, for to imagine is also to expose oneself to accusations of naivety or impracticality. Yet history suggests that what begins as impractical often becomes common sense once acted upon. The same might be true of a future where unpredictability is valued, convenience is tempered, and freedom is redefined not as escape from systems but as conscious navigation within them.

In the end, a new civic imagination is not about returning to some lost ideal of unmediated autonomy but about recognising that the future of freedom depends on our capacity to collectively reshape the systems in which we are embedded. It demands that we stop asking only how to resist within the digital order and begin asking what kind of order we want instead. It demands that we defend not just privacy but unpredictability, not just the individual but the collective, not just rights on paper but practices in everyday life. *To preserve unpredictability may indeed be the last defence of freedom—but to cultivate it requires nothing less than reimagining the very meaning of civic life in the digital age.*

About the Author

Avery Grant writes at the intersection of technology, power, and everyday life, focusing on how digital systems shape behavior long before laws or force are involved. With years of work interviewing engineers, city officials, and civil liberties advocates across North America, Europe, and Asia, Grant maps the hidden incentives that turn platforms into instruments of governance. Their essays and briefings have informed civic groups, product teams, and policymakers looking for concrete ways to balance innovation with autonomy. Grant's guiding conviction is simple: freedom depends on understanding the code, markets, and institutions that train us to comply—often without noticing.

www.ingramcontent.com/pod-product-compliance
Lightning Source LLC
Chambersburg PA
CBHW062003250926
51852CB00008B/23
9789390349890